In the Church, Yet Bound!

Carla Conley

DIXON PUBLISHING

The Publishing Midwife
DixonPublishingCompany.com
Colorado • Louisiana • DC
Texas • India • Africa

515-99-BOOKS

Copyright © 2023 Carla Conley

All rights reserved. No part of this publication may be reproduced, stored in a retrieval system, or transmitted in any form or by any means – electronic, mechanical, photocopy, recording, or any other – except for brief quotations in printed reviews, without the prior permission of the author.

Cover design by Dixon Publishing

Editor: Beatrice Bruno

First Edition

Unless otherwise indicated, Bible verses are from the King James Bible

Printed in the United States of America

TABLE OF CONTENTS

ACKNOWLEDGMENTS 5

FOREWORD 7

Chapter 1 Who Fell Through the Cracks? 9

Chapter 2 It's A Set Up! 13

Chapter 3 Foundation Gone 23

Chapter 4 I'm Not Taking No More! 31

Chapter 5 Moment of Security 39

Chapter 6 Mama, Can You Hear Me? 45

Chapter 7 Hell to Deal With 51

Chapter 8 Get Out! 59

Chapter 9 Running for My Life 77

Chapter 10 Gifts and Calling! 85

Chapter 11 The Separation 89

Chapter 12 The Abused Becomes the Abuser 105

Chapter 13 No Good Thing in My Flesh 119

Chapter 14 Unnatural Affection 127

Chapter 15 A Plan of Assassination 135

Chapter 16 Lord, Why Me? 149

Chapter 17 This Was My Heart! 153

Chapter 18 Out of the Frying Pan into the Fire 161

Chapter 19 The Believer's Two Natures 175

Chapter 20 Complete Deliverance 179

Chapter 21 Healing the Real Man (The Wounded Spirit) 185

Chapter 22 My Stages of Deliverance 191

Chapter 23 God Remains Yet Faithful! 197

Author Bio 201

ACKNOWLEDGMENTS

Father God, thank You for bringing Your Man of God into my life. Pastor Aaron E. Conley, my gift from God: thank you for your financial contribution supporting my vision of writing this book. Thank you for encouraging me to finish this book. Most of all, though, thank you for loving me; thank you for caring for me; thank you for standing with me...in spite of me. I love you!

I am grateful to late-Pastor G.S. and O.B. Matthew of Shiloh M. B. Church of Barrett Station. Thank you both for being parents in my life in a season in which I so needed you.

Thank you, Sister Rosie Mae Armstrong, for opening your home to me and loving me in the Lord. I also want to thank the late Judy Armstrong for befriending me and never judging me despite my struggles.

I am so grateful to the late Apostle Marvin Boyd and his precious wife, Sister Kathleen Boyd who remains in my corner to this day. Thank you both for taking me into your home, for your patience through my deliverance. Thank you for loving me in spite of my sin and faults.

Pastor Betty Joyce Crowder, God's Word of Deliverance Apostolic Faith Church Incorporated: I thank God for you! Thank you for your prayers, your support in the process of my complete deliverance, and for teaching me about another dimension of prayer in the Holy Ghost.

My parents, James Williams, and Joyce D. Recard: Dad and Mom, thank you for allowing God to create me through you.

Evangelist Sabrina Baker: God gave me a true friend in you. Thank you for encouraging me, loving me, and pushing me to finish my book!

My Ghostwriter and Editor, Apostle Beatrice Bruno: You took the ball and ran with it! With much prayer and guidance by the Holy Spirit, you brought everything to complete order in my book. I am grateful.

My Publisher, Dr. Cenece Dixon and Dixon Publishing Company: You took upon yourself the sole task of putting my book on display so that men and women, boys, and girls, would have the opportunity to be completely set free from the bondage of Satan in the Name of Jesus! Thank you! I am so very grateful to you and your team!

As you all know, the highest and best acknowledgment and gratitude goes to our Father Who Art in Heaven: Father God, His Son and our Lord and Savior, Jesus Christ, and His Precious Holy Spirit. Father God, thank You for Your patient tutelage. You deserve all the honor and credit as You led, directed, and brought all things back to my remembrance of whatever You commanded me to do on this path You created specifically for me. Thank You, my Triune God in Three Persons – Father, Son, Holy Spirit, for bringing me through and keeping me. I love You with ALL my heart!

Sincerely, Evangelist Carla (Beaver) Conley

FOREWORD

Carla Antoinette Beaver-Conley, whom I call my daughter in the Lord, is known for her straight-to-the-gut truth, her kind heart, and her strong work ethic. I've known her for over 30 years, and she lived in our home for 5 years. So, I know her!

Carla has always been very respectful, truthful, and kind-hearted. While living with us, she kept our home impeccable, cooked delicious meals, and helped us with our four growing sons. We loved her as if she was family because she was!

My husband, the late Apostle Marvin T. Boyd Sr., and I were Carla's Pastors. We served in a thriving church in Baytown, Texas, back in the mid 80's and 90's. **Truth** and **Love** connected us: *Truth* because, with Carla... you'll know the truth and nothing but the truth: so, help you God! *Love* because, with the type of heart Carla has, she never means any harm: she always wants to help if she can.

In Carla's book, ***In the Church Yet Bound***, Carla shares portions of her journey during which we walked with her. From her confession to us of her problem, to seeing her freed from her problem, we walked with Carla. And it took her <u>**choosing**</u> to walk in her freedom. She shared the pain with us; we shared our tears, our prayers, fasting, and the casting out of spirits with her through Christ! We never shared any of Carla's journey or what she was going through with anyone all these years: we just loved her through it!

In *In the Church Yet Bound,* you'll get it all... The Good, The Bad, and The Ugly! Carla will tell you! Carla is a viable source of energy. Although she will help you with her candid style, you will not feel condemned because she puts herself in your place. And along with Jesus, she'll help to lift you out of the muck and mire!

As you read *In the Church Yet Bound,* open your heart, and take every word to heart. These words, along with the Word of God, will help you get to that place of healing and peace in Christ Jesus!!

Minister Carla worked valiantly with the youth in our Church as well as with our music department. She also worked as a heart-warming nanny in our home. She went on even further by becoming a prayer warrior, a teacher of God's Word, and a profound speaker and Minister of the Gospel. Throughout all her trials, Carla has become a beautiful woman of God! And now, she is the wife of one of our favorite sons in the Lord, an awesome man of God!

Honored to be Minister Carla's spiritual Mother, I am also honored to have been her closest confidant and friend all these years! Until, of course, her husband, Brother Aaron, came... Now, he is the most special person to her!

So, I leave you with this: as you read *In the Church Yet Bound,* **PUT YOUR SEATBELT ON**!!! And may **GRACE** grab you!!

In HIS Will!

Kathy Boyd

In Honor of my late, Great Husband of almost 41 years, Apostle Marvin T. Boyd Sr.!

Much Love, Peace, and Blessings!!

Chapter 1

Who Fell Through the Cracks?

At the age of 23, Bessie Brown was the mother of seven children. On September 11, 1961, at Charity Hospital in New Orleans, Louisiana, Bessie gave birth to twins during Hurricane Carla. As a result of being in the Hurricane, the twins were named Carl and Carla.

I am Carla. To understand my story, this information is important.

In the book, "Healing the Wounded Spirit," John and Paula Sandford say that dogs will nose and push against the hands of people to ask for petting and stroking. I have often wondered why they become so insistent. What did it mean to them, or do for them, that made them press us for more and more? What was that thing inside of them that caused them to seek petting and stroking from humans?

Then the Lord revealed to me that He had given dogs a spirit which can feel our human spirits cascading in heaping waves of glory through their bodies when our hands stroke them.

Perhaps the smile is inept, but infants and young children also retain that same sensitivity. Their little spirits are open and vulnerable. They are present and able to melt into us or drink our presence through our touch. Every nursing mother knows that her baby drinks far more than milk from her.

When affection is given in normal, healthy ways, human spirits stay whole and seek normal, healthy ways of expression. When affection is not given, drives and urges express themselves in wrong ways. The spirit sickens, seeking out wrong answers for right needs.

True affection does not lead to improper sexual touch and embrace, but away from it. Unfortunately, the rare touch of inadequate affection turns into lust.

In wholesomely affectionate homes, all the forms of child abuse almost never manifest themselves. We do not need to fear touch; only the absence of it. When children have not received enough affectionate touch, it is the task of counselors and the Body of Christ to heal.

Affection given to a 50-year-old can warm the heart of the five-year-old within. When questions in counseling reveal starvation diets of affection, their inner child is willing to forgive. Never mind that the person's mind never has consciously identified resentment or anger. Our personal spirit has a mind of its own: it has desires which, when they are thwarted, turn to anger.

This becomes clear because, as a newborn, I was not given the love and affection I needed or desired from my daddy, Jimmy Paul, and my mama, Bessie Brown. Having a total of four little children, which now included twins, it was hard for Mama to give love and affection to so many who needed love and affection. Someone had to fall through the cracks. I was one of those *someone's*.

According to Mama, my twin, Carl, demanded more attention than I did. Mama assured me that I was a good baby: she fed and dressed me, and then put me back in my crib.

To confirm this information, Daddy shared that he used to tell Mama that she needed to put Carl down and hold me sometimes. Our Aunt Renell also shared that she used to come over, sometimes just to hold me.

Although I was born full-term, I only weighed four pounds. As a result, according to Mama, I had to stay in the hospital for a week after birth.

The following is from Medical News Today and speaks about babies born with low birthweight.

"A very low birth weight 'may increase risk of later-life psychiatric problems.' Babies with a very low birth weight may be at much higher risk of depression, ADHD, or other psychiatric conditions in adulthood, compared with those born at a healthy weight. Steroid use just before birth may increase this risk even further. This is according to a new study published in the journal *Pediatrics*.

"Past studies have established that babies with a low birth weight are at increased risk of numerous health problems later in life, including obesity, hypertension, diabetes and heart disease. But how does low birth weight affect mental health in adulthood?

"Very low birth-weight babies are up to 4.5 times higher at risk of psychiatric problems.

"To find out, Dr. Van Lieshout and his team analyzed the presence of psychiatric disorders among 84 adults who were born at an extremely low birth weight (less than 1,000 g) and 90 adults who were born at a normal birth weight. All participants were born between 1977 and 1982 in Ontario, Canada, and were in their early 30s at the time of assessment. The researchers found that the participants with an extremely low birth weight were three times less likely to develop a substance or alcohol use disorder than those with a normal birth weight.

"However, low-birth-weight participants were 2.5 times more likely to develop a psychiatric disorder in adulthood – such as depression, ADHD (attention deficit hyperactivity disorder) and

anxiety than those born at a normal weight, according to the team. (https://www.medicalnewstoday.com)"

In 1969, our family moved to Texas. At the time, my body could not stand getting too hot. When I got too hot, I would get sick and suffer from diarrhea. When these episodes occurred, I would also faint. The doctor diagnosed me with a nervous condition. I did not discover

I had this condition until I had a nervous breakdown while driving to work one day. I blanked out and ran into a light pole at a four-light stop sign.

My medical history is proof that the information about low-weight babies having short and long-term problems in life is correct.

These are some of the chronic conditions I deal with as an adult:

Right Bundle Branch Block	Fibromyalgia	Benign Ovarian Cyst
Obstructive Sleep Apnea (OSA)	BI	UI
Chronic Depression	Osteoarthritis	Internal Hemorrhoid
Diverticulitis	Hiatal Hernia	Impaired Hearing
Anxiety Arthritis	Gastroesophageal Reflux Disease – GERD	Hypercholesterolemia
Seasonal Allergies	Diabetes Mellitus Type 2	Cyst of Pancreas

Even now, after all these years and for no apparent reason, I will start having diarrhea and vomiting. I have had numerous tests performed and completed. The medical community still has not found what causes my body to react in this way. In addition, also for no apparent reason, my feet and skin peel in the same manner as a snake.

Only by the grace of God am I able to withstand these attacks on my body. I continue to live in this season of my life for His glory and for my good.

Chapter 2

It's A Set Up!

Life really began for me in 1969 when Daddy moved our family to Texas to live in Barrett Station after my grandmother passed.

Daddy had us all fooled into believing we were going to move into this big, two-story house. Just before we moved to Texas, he showed us a draft of the house we were going to live in: each of us would have our own bedroom; there was a playroom; and three bathrooms. Mama and daddy would have a big master bedroom. There was a big kitchen, and a room added on the outside supposedly to be a place for a washer and dryer.

We were told all this just to find out it was all a big lie.

Daddy loaded everything we had on a big U-Haul truck. Remember the bed rack the mattress lays on? That's what Daddy used to put behind the truck to lock us in and keep us cool for the ride. It was kind of fun, though, because we had never traveled before as children.

Uncle Don decided to ride with us, which was a good thing. Daddy had a sleep disorder; he would fall asleep at the drop of a hat regardless of whether he was behind the wheel or not.

Can you imagine our surprise as we pulled up to a two-story, green shack with four or five dogs barking at us? We were just little children along for the ride. Never having had pets before, at least that was a little exciting.

Then, we heard voices screaming, "Jimmy! Jimmy!"

The voices were coming at us from down St. Globe Street. We were not aware that this was our Daddy's mother, Lula Mae; his brother, Paul; his sisters, Lena, and Diana; and his cousins, Jacob, and Darrell.

When they got closer to us, we got scared. We kind of withdrew to Mama and Uncle Don. We had never met people who were mentally and physically retarded. This was also Mama's first-time meeting Daddy's family.

Daddy introduced his mother and family members to us. They were different from us. Their bodies were deformed; they were physically **and** mentally retarded. When they came up to us to tightly hug us, we were afraid of these new family members we had never met before.

Our Grandmother, Mother Dear, had long, pretty hair. I remember going to her house and combing her hair. She fell asleep every time. Mother Dear was such a sweet woman. I loved being around her and doing things for her.

Our life as children living in Barrett Station with Daddy was a hard life. In addition to not having water in our house, there was only one bathroom in the entire house. In addition to one bathroom without water, both were downstairs.

When we first moved there, we had to go around the corner to Mama Dock's house to get buckets of water so we could have water to cook, drink, take baths, and flush the commode.

Daddy and Mama slept in the master bedroom. All the children slept in the second bedroom downstairs. Carl and I were two when we moved to Texas. Since we were all small, I guess five girls and four boys sleeping in the same room was not so bad. And yes, some of us had to sleep on a mattress on the floor.

None of the rooms upstairs were finished. Daddy had a big board nailed to the wall that was supposed to be a door. The house was green on the outside. On one side of the house, you could see where he had nailed some boards together so he could stand on them to work on the house. He never finished the house.

Mama cooked on a big wood stove that stood in the middle of the floor. This same wood stove kept the whole downstairs very warm for the winter. We chopped wood to burn it in the stove. It did not matter to Daddy who chopped the wood as long as there was wood to burn. Eventually, the girls even learned to chop wood. In the winter, we had to make sure we chopped enough wood for the stove to keep the whole house warm.

We had some very cold winters there in Barrett Station. None of us wanted to go out and chop wood in the cold. Sometimes, though, only Daddy or one of my brothers went out and chopped the wood. Like I said earlier, though, the girls learned to chop wood as well.

During the summertime, Daddy had a big, big fan in the house; it cooled the whole downstairs. Sometimes, though, it was still hot in the house. All we could do was suffer through the heat while in the house. Since we were always playing outside, we really didn't mind the heat outside as much.

Many times, when Daddy woke us up in the morning for school, some of us had wet the bed. We would have to fill the tub with cold water. First, we would boil the water in the tub on top of the wood stove. Then, we would add soap-powder to the water. Daddy would have us get in the tub and stomp those soiled sheets until the scent of urine was out of them. We then took a bath in cold water before we dressed for school and after we washed the sheets.

As children, we didn't know what it meant to sleep in on Saturdays. Daddy woke us up early on Saturday mornings so we could clean and get the house in order. My little brother, James, and little sister, Liz, were too young at the time to do housework, but they were given chores and assignments to do as well.

We cleaned the house from top to bottom. We had an old washing machine with rollers. We put the clothes between those two rollers and turned the handle until it flattened the cloth, and all the excess water was out of the clothes. We even used a scrub board on some of the clothes.

When we hung the clothes on the clothesline, those white clothes were pure: white as snow. We also cleaned where the rabbits and chicken lived and fed them as well as part of our chores.

Daddy hauled junk. My brothers - Bob, Joel, and Carl - worked by stripping the cars Daddy received as junk. If our dogs had bad skin, Daddy would rub them down with the old oil from the cars he received. He would rub the oil all over the dog's fur, making sure it got down to their skin. After a few days, our dog's fur would return to normal, and it was beautiful!

We fed the dogs all the leftover food from the kitchen. Daddy would put everything into a big pot and cook everything together. The dogs would go crazy from the smell! They barked until the food cooled down and Daddy fed them.

Living with Daddy was something we were not accustomed to doing. It was like living in slavery. All the clothes we wore were hand-me-downs. I do not recall ever going to a store to shop for clothes.

There was an added room outside behind the house. I think it was maybe going to be a washroom. Just like everything else, though, it was never finished. I don't think anyone could have ever prepared us for what we had to do in **that** room.

One day, Daddy had us go and get plenty of buckets. He brought us out to the septic tank. Daddy took the cement lid off that tank and, OH, the horrible smell! We all began to get sick to our stomachs.

I won't use the word Daddy said, but he told us, "This is your mess, and the commode is backed up."

We had to carry those buckets into the woods and dump them. Daddy got in that septic tank and dipped those buckets in that mess. We carried them into the woods until the septic tank was empty.

As I mentioned earlier, Daddy made his living collecting and selling junk. My three brothers helped Daddy separate the iron, aluminum, metal, and copper from the junk he collected so he could sell those items.

When it was time to load the truck to go and sell the junk, my oldest brother rode inside the truck with Daddy. Joel and Carl rode on top of the junk in the back of the truck. Many times, because Daddy would fall asleep while driving, Bob had to wake him up because he would be all over the road. There were times my brother's lives were in danger because Daddy would almost go over the nearby cliffs.

We did our own landscaping. We cut the grass, pulled the weeds out of the flower beds, turned the dirt over to plant flowers, and put bricks around the flower beds.

When we were children, we were not required to go to church. On Sundays, or when it was convenient, Daddy sat us down at the table and had Bible Study with us.

Daddy raised himself. As a result of all he went through with his family, Daddy was an angry young man. At a young age, Daddy had to take care of himself. Daddy did not have a relationship with his Daddy. He was not close to his family at all. Which probably explains why he treated us the way he did: there was not really much love in his life.

Daddy was angry about how his family had treated his Mama. I believe that is why he did not know how to show any affection to us. When he beat us, he used sting cords, fan belts, broom sticks, and willow tree branches. Daddy seemed so hard at those times. He would beat us until our bodies were bruised. Despite the many times, I had to be beaten for something I should not have done, I had love for my dad.

One time, I decided to run away from home because I was tired of how Daddy handled us. I packed some clothes, rolled them up in a shirt, and took my baby doll with me. I sat under the canal for some hours. Not once did Daddy try to find me. I guess he already knew that when it got dark, I would head back home. We were so scared of our dad; he beat us so hard.

When it started getting dark, yes, I got scared and decided I had better go back home. Daddy was waiting for me at the front door. He lifted me up on my two legs and beat me for running away.

I screamed, "I love you, Daddy," over and over.

He said, "I love you, but you're still getting this *blank* beating. You want to run away again?"

I said, "No, Daddy."

He let me down with bruises all over my legs. Mama was not pleased with how Daddy disciplined us. I am sure she said some things about it, but never in our presence.

I will say this: our parents never argued in front of us. I guess when they went into their room, all hell probably broke loose.

My siblings and I were very close. Although we had friends in school, Daddy would not let us go and play at their homes. Our friends never played at our house, either. So, we learned to play with each other. We could not spend the night with our friends. As a result, we were very resourceful. We made our own go-kart ride; the ditches were our swimming pool.

For some reason, Daddy thought that doing this next thing was fun. He would wait until it got dark and then convince us that he was taking us for a ride. And he would: he would drive us right into the graveyard, drunkenly jump out of the truck, and leave us there, screaming and hollering.

After a while, he always came back and got us. We were not happy with what he did to us. I have no idea why we kept getting in that truck with Daddy. We knew the same thing would happen again. One time, I guess my oldest brother, Bob, got tired of Daddy leaving us in the graveyard for the last time. He got behind the wheel and drove us back home. Daddy never took us to the graveyard again.

Daddy was friends with two elderly women: Miss O'Bryant and Miss Roberta. I would go over there with him when he spent time with them. While he was talking with them, I would play with Sheila, their granddaughter, until Miss Roberta found some work for me to do.

Miss Roberta would work me hard while I was there. I climbed the trees in her yard, picked all the figs, and put them in a bucket. She paid me a quarter regardless of how much work I did. I always thought she could have given me a little more than a quarter.

On another day, I had to pull the whole rug up from the dining room floor and replace it with the other carpet she had. I was so tired by the time I finished the assignment. She paid me with a one-liter coke. I loved Miss O'Bryant and Miss Roberta: they were some sweet, old women. I sometimes sat and listened to them tell their stories. Some of their stories were very funny.

One day, Miss O'Bryant saw a snake in her house. Daddy went over there and found that long snake. He had me stay with her at night for a while until she was comfortable by herself again.

I will never forget the Christmas of 1970. I was telling my brothers and sisters to be thankful for whatever gifts they got because God did not have to bless us with anything. As everyone received their presents and opened them, Mama gave me this small present wrapped in red paper. I opened the present with tears in my eyes. It was a little square puzzle I had to move around to get all the pieces back in place. I cried as I looked at the big gifts the rest of my siblings had.

Everyone looked at me and sarcastically said, "You need to be thankful for what God blessed you with; you did not have to get anything."

That only made it worse. I did not understand why my present was something I did not believe was a girl's present. Why did I not get a doll like my other sisters did? That was the only Christmas I remember when Daddy was at home with us.

Daddy was a character. He could fix and do anything. One day, the light company came and turned our lights off. Daddy waited until they left, got on that light pole, and turned our lights back on.

There is one situation, though, I will never forget.

Daddy would do some of the craziest things. He would do things like drink his drink half-way and put hot sauce in it just to see if he could catch one of us drinking his drink. One day, he was eating a sausage. He had a small piece left and put that piece into the icebox. He then went outside to do some work.

Joel, one of my older brothers, went in and ate the small piece of sausage. Daddy came in and went straight to the icebox, looking for his sausage. He knew it was only a matter of time before one of us took it.

He asked, "Who ate my sausage?"

None of us answered; we knew he would beat whoever ate that sausage.

Finally, he said, "OK, I'm going to beat all of you."

Because we feared Daddy and his beatings, we told him, "Joel ate your sausage."

Daddy got that sting cord. He beat Joel until some of his skin peeled off. We were all scared and crying; Daddy seemed like he was never going to stop beating Joel. Finally, though, he let Joel go.

When Mama came home, she asked, "What is wrong?"

We were all still crying and pointed to Joel. Daddy had beaten our brother like an animal. Some of his skin had broken apart.

We all cried as Mama put medicine on Joel's bruises. She went into her and Daddy's room; boy, was she mad. We do not know what took place behind that closed door, but Daddy never beat us in that way again.

One time, Daddy and Mama were in their room with the door closed. I knocked on the door several times. I thought I heard Daddy say, "Come in."

I opened the door. Very quickly, this steel-toed boot hit me right in the face, knocking me to the floor.

Daddy said, "What do you want?"

I was crying because he had just hit me in the face with a steel-toed boot. My head was hurting.

I told him, "Nothing."

He said to me, "Yes, you want something."

After that boot hit me, I could not remember what I wanted. From that point, though, Daddy made me knock on their door using the knot on my head, crying.

Brenda, my oldest sister, was an incredibly quiet person. She never gave Mama any problems. A little on the heavy side, she was able to carry a baby for nine months without anyone questioning her weight. When it was time for the baby to come, Brenda complained of a headache. Mama, unaware of what was really going on, was trying to give Brenda something for her head.

Daddy finally told Mama, "Brenda is pregnant, and the baby is coming now."

Daddy and Mama rushed Brenda to the hospital; she had a baby boy.

In all of what we went through with the hardness of Daddy, he never hugged us. He never really showed any affection to us. To be honest, I do not even remember Mama hugging me or showing any affection. I would not know until later in life how that affected me and how I would connect with others.

Chapter 3

Foundation Gone

In 1971, Daddy left.

I remember the many times my parents had their best friends over: Mr. Dock and his wife Ellen; Mr. Simon and his wife Dora. They drank liquor. Mama and Mrs. Ellen smoked cigarettes and drank. They all listened to 60's and 70's music. Daddy especially loved listening to B.B. King.

Back in those days, children were not allowed to be in the grown-up's faces. Daddy and Mama and their friends played cards and Dominoes. Daddy would hit those Dominoes on that table so hard, the whole table shook. Daddy was so loud, and he would use cuss words most of the time. The way Daddy talked so much noise while playing the game, you would have thought he created the game of Dominoes.

While the grown-ups enjoyed their games and talking, we played with their children outside. The only time we went through those doors was to use the restroom or get some water; and then, only by permission. These two couples were friends with my parents for many years.

As I indicated earlier, children were not involved in grown-up problems and affairs. Five of Mama's children were not Daddy's biological children. However, all of them knew him to be their

Daddy.

Can you imagine how we felt as children? Our Daddy was leaving us, and we did not know why. Back in those days, children were not involved in grown-up business and were not even part of the conversations. All we knew was that our Daddy was leaving us: that was all we needed to know.

Whatever went on behind closed doors stayed behind closed doors when it came to grown-ups. We knew Daddy had left, but we did not know at the time why he left. Neither did we know who he had left with at that time. We found out later that Daddy took Mrs. Ellen Dock, Mama's best friend, his best friend's wife, and her children. They moved to Tulsa, Oklahoma.

When Daddy, the head of our household, left our home, we no longer had a foundation to stand on. In Scripture, the very basic scriptures show that the man is the head, the one who holds everything up.

According to https://www.houzz.com, in many respects, the foundation is the most important element of any building, whether it is a house or a high-rise. The man in the house, then, is the glue that holds all things together according to the Word of God.

Ephesians 5:23 KJV makes it clear who should be the head of a household according to God's design for the family. *For the husband is the head of the wife, even as Christ is the head of the church: and he* (Jesus) *is the Saviour of the body.*

We err when we disregard all the aspects of headship. A head cannot function on its own. It is as dependent on the rest of the body as the body is dependent on the head. God is careful to define leadership by comparing it to Christ's love for the church and Him giving Himself for the church. (**See Ephesians 5:25 – 30**)

I was 14 when Daddy removed himself from our home. After he left, I began experiencing major behavioral problems under the authority of Mama and all other authorities. I was giving Mama an extremely hard time. If Mama wanted me to go right, I went left. If she wanted me to go left, I went right.

Even though Daddy had been giving me terrible beatings, I was still closer to him than to Mama. I never knew the reason until much later in life as an adult. I did not want my Daddy to leave me.

On the day he left, I fell to the ground and grabbed his leg. I cried, "Daddy, do not leave! Please."

He said, "I got to, Baby."

"No, Daddy. Please do not leave me. I love you."

"I love you, too, Baby."

He left with Mrs. Ellen and her children. I wonder how Mrs. Ellen's children felt as they left their Daddy during this time, especially with their Daddy's best friend.

Mama stayed in the street after Daddy drove off. My brothers and sisters walked in the street with Mama, trying to calm her down.

As a result of Daddy leaving, Mama had to get a job. She found a job cleaning the house of a Caucasian family. She also took care of their three children: Katie, Jack, and Betty. In addition to that, she also worked at a small burger place called *Snack Shack*.

My oldest sister, Brenda, helped take care of us and her baby boy, Michael, while Mama worked. Brenda never really had an opportunity to enjoy her childhood; she had helped raise her younger brothers and sisters.

During this time, my brothers, Joel and Carl, often got into confrontations with each other. Many times, Brenda had to stand between them to try to stop them from hurting each other.

While Daddy lived with us, we seemed to be closer to each other. All of that changed when he left. Mama was more distant from us; it affected each of us in different ways.

Each of my siblings went into survival mode; we all separated from each other. You would have thought that the trauma of Daddy leaving would have brought us closer together. That was not the case. Our lives changed dramatically after Mama went to work to provide for us.

Daddy never sent Mama anything to help take care of his children. Yes, I know that not all my siblings were his birth children; but Daddy was the only Daddy they knew. During all this time, though, and despite everything, Mama kept food on the table.

We didn't have clothes or toys like the other kids. We made our own toys. We wore whatever Mama provided for us. Regardless of whether the clothes were hand-me-downs from other people or whatever, I was not concerned about my clothing until I was around my peers.

My siblings and I played on the big piece of grassy property next door to our house. From our childhood perspectives, we thought that the grass was as high as the sky. We took big boxes, got inside of them, and rolled in that field of tall grass. We would crush the grass down, making a trail so we could play. At this time in my life, I was mostly withdrawn from the others. I played by myself most of the time.

I made my own doll house. I pretended I was in a luxury home that I owned. I would sing, believing that one day I would be a Gospel singer. Very tomboyish, I used to climb up those big trees, all the way to the top, and scream loudly so the entire world could hear me.

I am not proud to even speak about the things I started doing after Daddy left. To be transparent in this book and in life, I have decided to leave no rocks unturned in my life. The enemy has been holding this over my head ever since I gave my life to Jesus Christ in September 1979.

I was between 14 and 15 when Daddy left and moved to Tulsa. I wasn't brought up in a Godly home. No one taught me how to do what I am about to tell you about. Nor had I seen another person do what I was doing.

Living in the country and because I was such a tomboy, I had many cuts on my body. Those cuts became sore. One day while I was sitting outside on the ground, our dog Spot came over to me. I hugged Spot and gave him some love. I had a big sore on my leg; Spot began to lick my sore. At first, I tried to make him stop. But I remembered that I had heard that when a dog licks a person's sore, something in his saliva helps heal the sores.

I started allowing Spot to lick my sores. And really and truly, the sores were healing. But Spot began trying to bite the scab off my sores. That was not good because the sores weren't healed beneath the scab. I stopped him from licking my sore.

After stopping Spot from licking my sores, he began trying to lick between my legs. At first, I pushed Spot away. But something inside of me said, "Try it and see how it feels."

I decided to try it out. I pulled my panties to the side and allowed Spot to lick my private areas. Soon, I began to receive sexual gratification from what Spot was doing. At times, I got mad with Spot because he had other things catching his attention, and he didn't want to lick my privates.

I would push his nose and mouth to make him lick my privates. Sometimes I was successful. Then, there were times when Spot became angry with me, and I had to let him go about his business.

During this time, I was still going over to Miss Roberta and Miss O'Bryant's house, helping them as much as I could. Miss Roberta worked me like I was a Hebrew slave. I climbed those trees to pull all the figs off so she could make fig preserves. Sometimes, I ate more figs than I put in the bucket; Miss Roberta didn't mind because I was at least getting the job done.

Just like before, I would have to pull all the carpet off the living room floor and drag it out of the house to the back to be burned on the trash pile. Afterward, I installed the new carpet. My pay never got any higher. I would be paid either a one-liter Coke or 25 cents.

One day when I was at their house playing dolls with Sheila and combing their hair, Miss Roberts saw that I had started my period. I do not believe Mama had talked to me about having a period. Miss Roberta told me to go home to Mama.

I saw the blood in the center of my panties. I did not know what was happening to me. You know the *Girl Talk* your mom should have with you to prepare you for this time in your life? Well, Mama did not have that *Girl Talk* with me.

I ran home, making sure no one saw me. I went to the bathroom and stuffed my panties with toilet paper in an effort to try to stop the bleeding. I never told Mama or my sisters what was going on with me. I just kept on stuffing my panties with toilet paper.

The next day, I wore yellow pants to school. I thought I had stuffed my panties well, but the blood kept coming out of me. Mrs. Debra, the PE teacher, saw the blood. She took me to the side and told me to go home, and she would tell the office.

I ran all the way home. I felt so ashamed and wondered when this bleeding was going to stop. After three days, I finally stopped bleeding. I was so relieved! I wasn't aware that this cycle would happen every month. Between 1972 and 1973, the children at school made fun of how I dressed and smelled.

This one girl, Debbie Clark, picked on me and made fun of me every day. At that time, I feared Debbie Clark. Between the 4th and 6th grades, I didn't give my teacher any problems; I was a good student. In the 7th and 8th grades, though, things changed.

I will never forget the day we were de-segregated.

In June 1972, White children had to come to Barrett Schools; the Black children had to go to Crosby School. It was not a smooth transition. We did not want to go to Crosby, and they did not want to come to Barrett Station.

Chapter 4

I'm Not Taking No More!

In 1974, all I heard Mama saying to me was, "You are bad; you are stubborn; you are hardheaded!"

These were things I repeatedly heard in my ear.

Every time Mama was going to beat me for something I had done wrong, I ran from her. I would run upstairs and hide in the closet. When she came upstairs and found me, I always managed to slip away from her. I would move that big board covering the open door and jump down from our two-story house and fall on the ground without a scratch.

Day or night, I would run through the grass away from Mama.

She would tell me, "You have to come back."

My sister Brenda would wait until Mama was in her room and give me supper. I would wait until Mama went to sleep, then climb up on the side of the house using the ladder Daddy had built on the side of the house he had never finished.

Mama became very frustrated with me running from her. So, when it was time for a beating from her, she would have my brother Bob grab me before I took off. One time, she tied me to a tree and beat me while the rooster pecked at my legs.

I will never forget the time when Mama tied me to the bed to beat me. As she beat me, I managed to loosen the rope she had tied to the bed. I jumped quickly from the bed, grabbed the door knob, and pulled the door halfway before Mama shut my neck in the door. I remember seeing blood coming from my nose.

I said to her, "Mama, you are going to kill me. You just wait!"

I guess she finally got tired of beating me that evening.

The next day, my brothers, sisters, and I went out to play in the vacant lot next to our house. Although we were very poor, we were also very resourceful. We continued to make our own toys.

To this day, I have no idea where we obtained those huge boxes we used to play in that empty lot. The lot was not maintained, so we had the run of it. That grass was so high, you could get lost, and no one could find you. We had so much fun rolling around in those boxes as we made walking trails through that lot.

One day, my next oldest sister, Esther, was down on St. Charles Street playing with Jean and Betsy. After I left the vacant field, I saw Esther across the street with her friends. I walked across the street to her.

They wanted me to play this game with them called *Make the Sandwiches*. I told my sister I didn't want to play that game. They kept pushing me to play the game, so I did.

Esther was the bottom slice of bread; Jean was the meat; Betsy was the cheese; Dorothy was the lettuce and tomato; I was the last slice of bread.

I finally got off and said, "I don't feel right playing this game," and left.

One day, Esther was going to a friend's house. I wanted to follow her, but she told me I couldn't. I knew she would beat me up if I didn't turn back and head home. I waited until I thought she couldn't see me. I ran to catch up but stayed far behind so she couldn't see me. Esther went through the graveyard and went to the Blackwell trailer house. I saw her knocking on the door; someone let her in.

I waited for about 20 minutes, then went and knocked on the door. Jennifer opened the door. I asked if Esther was there.

She told me, "Yes."

I went in. Esther came out of the room with Joy. She was mad at me for following her. She told me to go back home. I told her I was going to tell Mama.

Esther told me to sit on the sofa and not to move. I knew something was not right because they all went back into the room. Esther never said a word to me about it after we went home. I never told Mama. At that time, I didn't know Esther liked girls.

Mama became friends with Mrs. Debra Jefferson who lived down the street from us. Every morning, Mama would go and drink coffee with Mrs. Jefferson. Mrs. Jefferson had five sons: Larry, Carlton, Brian, Dave, and Darryl. She had two daughters: Joy and Jennifer. The Jefferson's always thought they were better than our family because we did not live in a brick home and were not able to have nice things like them.

The Jefferson's also thought they were goodie-two-shoes. They would say mean things to us, and we would meet down the street from the house to fight. Bob, my oldest brother, would fight Carlton, their oldest son; Joel would fight Dave; I would fight Darryl and Larry at the same time.

Jefferson's daughter, Joy, did not live with them. She occasionally came over and visited Mrs. Debra and her stepdad, Mr. Cedrick.

Jennifer, their other daughter, became Bob's girlfriend. Bob played football at Bert High School; he was a great football player.

One day as I was walking down the street near Jennifer's house, she began talking about my Mama. I became very angry with her.

I went over to Jennifer, balled up my fist, and hit her in the face. I was so angry with Jennifer. I beat her until she was screaming and hollering. Jennifer ran into her house,

Mrs. Jefferson came out and told me, "Come here."

She was going to give me a beating. I told her she was not going to touch me and ran home.

Two weeks later, I was going to the Bellow house. Debbie Clark lives on the end of the other street by the Bellow house. When we were in elementary school, Debbie would talk about me, and her friends would laugh at me. My siblings and I did not dress in name brand clothes. This caused others to make fun of me, of us. I would just keep on walking, too scared to defend myself.

On that day, though, I had a tree branch in my hand. The branch had a long, pointed sticky stem on the end. Debbie's street and Bellow's Street connected. Both families were sitting on their porches.

By now, Debbie and I were both in high school. I wasn't that same scared little girl from elementary school.

No one knew then that I was carrying a weapon I had made with my own hands, hidden in a belt. I also had a knife in my sock. I had taken a big belt and opened the seams in the middle of the belt. I had put a chain inside of the belt, added some extra material, and sewed the seam back together. No one would know I was carrying any type of weapon unless I had to pull the weapon out.

Debbie was on the porch of her house. She came out to show off in front of her family. She came up to me while I had this stick branch in my hand. Even though the branch did not touch her, she said it did. I became very angry. Debbie had been a thorn in my flesh since we were in elementary school.

I said to her, "I did not touch you! Now what? I am not that scared little girl in elementary school that you made fun of with your friends."

Debbie pushed me. Before I knew it, I pulled the knife out of my sock, grabbed Debbie around the neck, and told her I was going to slit her throat.

Debbie's Mama, sister, and brother were on their porch watching us. The Bellow family was on their porch watching.

Everyone ran because they heard Debbie screaming, "She has a knife! She is going to kill me!"

I said to her, "I am tired of you messing with me. I was not bothering you, and your family saw you come out and mess with me."

I could hear Helena, Lula, and Rhonda's voices, "No, Carla, please."

Mother Jug finally came out to the street where I was holding Debbie. Mother Jug began talking to me.

Crying out of anger, I told Mother Jug, "I didn't stick her. She is lying like she always lies."

Mother Jug said, "Carla, let's go to the house. Take the knife off of Debbie's neck."

Debbie's family was screaming profanities. I continued to hold the knife at her neck.

I told them, "If any one of you comes close to me, you are going to have a dead daughter."

Mother Jug's voice calmed me down as she kept talking to me.

She slowly grabbed my other hand with affection and told me, "You do not want to do this. Give me the knife."

I pushed Debbie away from me. At that time, Debbie's family had moved back as Mother Jug asked them, but they were still cursing. I never had any problems out of Debbie from that day forward.

As I got older, my behavior got worse. During the summer, I climbed large trees all the way to the top, screaming out loud like I was King Kong. I also fought boys and anyone who messed with me. I did not take anything from anyone. I had gotten tired of letting people push me around until I went for blood.

One day, this girl Mary came to me to fight. She tried to act like she was so bad. It had just finished raining and the ditches were full of water. When she came at me, I threw her in a ditch full of water. I put her head under the water until she was kicking her legs to breathe. I did not care; I was going to teach her a lesson.

My sister saw Mary struggling to breathe. Mary was coughing hard from the water in her nose and mouth. After my sister pushed me off Mary and Mary started running home, I just laughed.

My sister said to me, "You are crazy."

I guess I was determined not to obey.

I was always catching a beating from Mama, though. I would make her angry while she was cooking dinner. Every day, as soon as she started preparing dinner for us, I would stand at the door of the kitchen like I was starving. Many times, she would tell me to go and sit down until she finished cooking.

When Mama fixed our plates, I had the most food. I was always hungrier than my siblings. Mama would fix a large plate of food for me; I would finish all my food and ask for more. This made her angry with me.

One time, though, Mama was determined to teach me a lesson. She put all the rest of the rice in the big pot in which she had cooked the white kidney beans. She told me to eat all that was in the pot. I was excited about eating some more food...Until my stomach began to fill up. I told Mama I had had enough.

Mama told me, "No, you are not full. Keep eating."

I said, "Yes, Mama. I am full."

I was so full; I started getting sick to my stomach and was about ready to throw up.

Mama said, "You better not throw up one piece of rice."

Feeling the weight of the threat, I finally finished eating the food in the pot.

Mama said, "That should teach you a lesson and stop you saying that you are not full."

On another day, I had done something for which I would receive a beat down. Mama was beating me with a sting cord. I ran upstairs and hid in a closet with no door in one of the rooms. Mama came up, found me, and hit me again. I ran out of the closet and removed the board covering the opening. I jumped down from the house and ran through the weeds.

I heard Mama say, "You must come back to this house."

I did not go back home that night; I went to a house that was being built. I went in through the window and found a liquor bottle. I saw some liquid still in the bottle. There were no lights in the house. As I lifted the bottle to drink the liquor, a cockroach floated into my mouth. I spit it out.

That night, I decided I was not going to listen to anybody.

I was called a tomboy because I played basketball with the boys in my community; I was good at basketball. When it came to picking the person to be on your team, I was always the first person everyone wanted on their team. They wanted me on their team.

Every day, a bunch of us walked to school together; I was a leader in the bunch. I was the school clown. Back in those days, though, teachers were allowed to paddle students. I was determined to not be pushed around by anyone or let anyone tell me what I could or could not do.

Mr. Thomas was my history teacher. Carla, the class clown, was not going to listen to any authority figures.

Mr. Thomas, a very big man, paddled me right in front of my friends.

Although those licks really hurt, they also made me that much angrier. I was a class clown. I did things in Mr. Thomas's class knowing that what I did would get me in trouble. But I also did it to get a response from my classmates.

Even though Mr. Thomas was a good teacher, something was driving me to not do what he asked; especially if it gave me the attention I craved.

My math teacher was an African American woman named Mrs. Katy. She did not play. And yet, I gave her trouble as well. Many times, she placed a desk outside of the classroom so I could do my homework and not interrupt the other students. Although she paddled me at times, I kept on doing what I wanted to do.

I am sure my teachers tried to get Mama to come up to the school. To my knowledge, she never showed up.

Mrs. Adams was my reading teacher. She had such a hard time getting me to do what she asked me to do, she finally quit teaching at the school.

I liked my Speech Therapy teacher, though. She was an African American woman and was very tender with me. I had a speech problem. I spent at least an hour in her class saying different words.

Because I was a distraction to other students, always saying things to make the class laugh or not doing my homework, I was assigned a special desk beside Principal Charles Guillory's office down the hall. I was a troubled child.

As some of my classmates came to the office for their teachers, I would clown with them until the principal would say, "Beaver! Alright!"

Several times, Mr. Don, my science teacher, paddled me. With all of the paddling, I cried. But that did not stop me from doing what I wanted to do.

Chapter 5
Moment of Security

In 1975, my brother Joel's best friend was Lionel. One day, Lionel asked Joel if he knew anyone that could help his Mama. Lionel's Mama had just had major surgery and needed someone to clean the house until she was able to get back on her feet. Lionel's Daddy, Pastor Paul, was a heavy smoker. He was diagnosed with emphysema and was on oxygen.

Joel told Mrs. Belinda, "My sister, Carla, loves to clean."

Joel then told me that Mrs. Belinda would pay me to come and help clean her house.

Pastor Paul and Mrs. Belinda Jackson lived on St. Charles Street down at the end of the road from our house. One day after school, Joel took me to meet the Jacksons. Joel rang the doorbell.

Lionel asked through the door, "Who is it?"

"It's Joel."

Lionel opened the door, "What's up, Man?"

"This is my little sister, Carla."

"Hi," I said.

Lionel let us in the house. Pastor Paul and Mrs. Belinda were watching the news on the television. Lionel introduced us to his parents.

After I said hello, Mrs. Belinda stood up and took me to each room of the house, telling me what she wanted me to clean. The Jackson's had a very lovely home. We then went to the laundry room where she informed me that she also wanted me to do their laundry.

We then went through the two-car garage to the big backyard. They had beautiful flowers and large trees in the backyard. There was also a nice outdoor table and chairs to sit on in the cool of the day.

I began going to Mrs. Belinda's house every day. I gathered all the dirty towels in the bathrooms, took the sheets off the beds, and started the wash before I began cleaning each room. Pastor Paul became used to me; he was so gentle and nice.

Mrs. Belinda went back to work as an RN at Saint Paul Hospital in Houston. She would get home at about 5:30 in the afternoon. Around that time, I was finishing up in her bedroom. When Mrs. Belinda came home, she spoke to her husband and me. Then, she would go into the kitchen to prepare dinner for her family.

I would finish folding and washing the rest of the clothes. Mrs. Belinda would ask me to stay and eat supper with them.

At that time, my Mama was either at work or at home. I really enjoyed being with Mrs. Belinda. We would play all kinds of games: Scrabble, Monopoly, and Checkers. I really did not like playing Scrabble because my spelling was not great. But Mrs. Belinda never made me feel bad.

My hair began falling out. Mrs. Belinda began braiding my hair so it would last a whole week for school. My hair grew so fast! Pretty soon, I had a big afro. I was so excited about my hair; it was starting to get long.

I was getting closer and closer to Mrs. Belinda. She showed me so much affection, it was hard not to love her. Mrs. Belinda told me how to carry myself around Lionel because he was a young man.

After school, I could not wait for Mrs. Belinda to get home. We usually went to the stores together. I finally met her family in Houston: Barbara Ann, her niece; Cecile and Terrie, her great nieces; Mrs. Tanner, her sister.

Mrs. Belinda's family was very nice to me. They made me fit right into their family. The money I made from the Jackson family was used by Mrs. Belinda to buy my school clothes and things a young lady needs monthly.

My affection for Mrs. Belinda was greater than any affection I had ever felt for Mama. I started going every morning to Mrs. Belinda's house before she went to work to get ready for school. Mrs. Belinda kept my clothes at her house. She finally asked Mama if I could come and live with them. Mama said yes.

Pastor Paul also said it was alright with him for me to live with them; that is if two women could live in the same house together.

For the first time in my life, I had a bed of my own, and a beautiful bedroom with everything a young lady could desire. The bedroom was luxurious, just like a dollhouse or from a story book. Mrs. Belinda talked to me about lady things, like what to do after I took my shower and put my robe and slippers on because we had men in the house. There was nothing I could not talk about with Mrs. Belinda. We talked about boys, sex, and how I should conduct myself as a lady.

When Mrs. Belinda came home in the afternoons and I finished cleaning, we sometimes sat in the backyard. I would tell her what my day at school was like.

Mrs. Belinda and her family were so kind to me. I truly felt like I was a part of a family for the first time.

I applied for a job at Wilson's Department Store in the Mall: I was hired. I was so excited! This was my first job at a department store. They taught me what I needed to do at the cash register. I was slow, but I still knew how to do the work. The only problem I had was that

I did not know how to count my register at night.

I was required to have $50 in my cash drawer, but I had to break it up. I did not know how to do that. I had to ask someone to please help me. Julie was genuinely nice and helped me every night. I felt so dumb. I shared this with Barbara Ann; she shared it with her mom, Mrs. Sharon.

On a Saturday when Mrs. Sharon and Barbara were at the house, they built a cash register and had about $1000 in it. They showed me how to count the money. Although it was hard at first, I kept trying every day until I was able to break the $50 down into smaller increments.

Even though I was slower than the other employees, I learned how to break up a $50 in the cash register: 1 - $20; 1 - $10; 2 - $5; 5 - $1; 8 – Quarters; 20 – Nickels; 100 – Pennies.

School was out and it was summer. Mama decided we were going to spend a month with Auntie Nealy in New Orleans.

I told Mama I did not want to go.

She said to me, "You do not have no wants."

I honestly believe she made me go because of the relationship I had with Mrs. Jefferson. I felt that she was making me go out of spite.

I cried to Mrs. Belinda and told her, "I do not want to leave." I wanted to stay with her.

She said, "I know. The days will go by fast and you will be back home."

When we made it to my Auntie Nealy and Uncle Dave's house, I was determined that I was not going to have a good time; I did not want to be there. One morning we were at the table eating breakfast. I was crying and Auntie Nealy asked what was wrong with me.

"I wanted to stay with Mrs. Jefferson," I answered.

Auntie Nealy told me that I loved that lady more than I loved my own Mama. She was right. I did not know why I did not feel close to Mama. I just felt that she did not love me because of the way she treated me.

The month ended. We were back home in Texas. I ran to Mrs. Belinda's house; I had missed her so much. When I got there, Mrs. Sharon and Barbara Ann were there. I was happy to see them, too. I was home again. We played Checkers and Scrabble and ate fried fish and French fries.

The Jacksons decided to go on a vacation. I was very hurt that they did not take me with them. Every day when I got out of school, I went down to their house, stood on a big board, and sang Gospel songs. I still believed I would one day be a Gospel singer for the Lord.

Even though she had never had children of her own, Mrs. Belinda was such a good mother to Lionel, whom she had adopted. I thought that life was going to stay the way it was...until Pastor Paul died.

I could tell that Mrs. Belinda missed Pastor Paul; I noticed the sadness in her eyes on many days. I became more involved in Anglo Missionary Baptist Church. I became so involved; Mrs. Belinda and I did not spend as much time together as we had before.

We both believed differently when it came down to the Bible. Mrs. Belinda never talked about the Word of God to me. There were times I would share things about the Word of God, but she never really responded. Afterward, I would try not to talk to her on that level. I believe this was one of the reasons we drifted apart. I still loved Mrs. Belinda, but things began changing in my life.

Mrs. Belinda sold her house and moved away. I did not know where because we had drifted apart. She never tried to contact me to tell me she was selling her house and moving away. One day, I went over there and discovered she had sold the house.

I never heard from Mrs. Belinda Jackson again.

Chapter 6

Mama, Can You Hear Me?

In the summer of 1976, I met Maryann. We both worked for the children's summer camp located at the back of the Drew Junior High School field. We were given all types of games and equipment for the children to play with.

Maryann was a few years older than me. She lived on Melvin Street, a block from my house; we became friends. Every day, I met Maryann at her house, and we walked up the road together to the field to meet the children.

After the summer program, I continued meeting Maryann at her house. In this season of my life, I always wore dark sunshades. Maryann's female family members always walked around the house in skirts that covered up their breasts. They had nothing else on but their panties.

One day, Maryann accused me of looking at her. I told her that I had not looked at her at any time in the way she was insinuating. I did not know that this was a type of her easing me into her world.

Maryann was a big girl. At this time, I did not go around looking at girls of any type in any way. What I didn't know was that the devil had set a trap for me. I was not saved and was not aware of his schemes.

Maryann and I became close friends. We both enjoyed helping the kids in the community. One thing I thought was good was that Maryann did not mind standing up for me, even with her family. One of Maryann's older sisters, Barbara, always had something negative to say about me. Whenever she did, Maryann stood up for me.

I cannot tell you why I agreed to this relationship with Maryann; I do not have an answer.

One day, Maryann asked me to meet her at midnight by the white car on the other side of her house. Inside of myself, I was afraid, but I also had an urge to do what Maryann told me to do.

When Daddy left us, I wanted to be by myself and have my own space. Even though the room upstairs was half finished, it didn't matter; I had my own room.

After my siblings and I ate supper and watched TV for a while, at 9 PM, we all had to go to bed. I went upstairs. I could hear Mama in the kitchen washing the dishes and putting the leftovers into the ice box. I could see Mama's shadow because the stairs from my room went down into the kitchen.

Because the kitchen light shined upstairs in my room, I knew when Mama finished what she was doing in the kitchen. When she turned off the kitchen light, my bedroom wasn't as bright. I never went to sleep with the lights off; I was afraid of the spiders that always came out of where Daddy didn't install the sheet rock. The spiders had webs on both ends of the corner and were hidden in the dark.

Around 11:45, I quietly went downstairs to see if everyone was asleep. I climbed out of a window on the side of the house where Daddy had left boards through which he could climb up and down. No one would ever know that I wasn't in my room. I climbed down to the side of the house, and quietly walked away from our home.

I started running on St. Charles Street until I made my way to Melvin Street where Maryann lived. I stood outside in the dark by the white car, waiting for Maryann to come out of her house. She finally came out of the house. She opened the car door, and we got in. She kissed me on the mouth, grabbed my right hand, and placed it inside her private area. Although I didn't feel right with what she made me do, I did it anyway.

Maryann and her older sister, Jolly, slept in the same bed. When Jolly awakened to find out that Maryann was not in bed, she said the Lord led her to come outside to the white car. When she looked inside the car and saw Maryann and me, she ran back to the house, screaming loudly.

Maryann told me not to worry, and to go home. She said she would take care of her sister and her family. I was scared and ashamed of what I had allowed Maryann to lead me to do. I ran home, climbed up those boards into the window, and got into bed. I was shaking because I knew that something about all of this was not right.

The next day as I was walking down the street, Maryann's sister Barbara saw me and screamed out of her window, "You are going to hell."

Every day after that encounter, if I saw any of their cars coming down the road, I jumped in the ditch, laid down, and hid. I was scared!

Barbara was friends with my Mama. She told Mama what had happened between Maryann and me. Mama never confronted me about what had taken place. Then, one day, she said that my siblings and I were going to spend the summer with Daddy.

After Daddy and Mama talked, I was told that Daddy went to the Bellow's house and told them, "Maryann has ruined my daughter Carla's life." He told them that he did not want Maryann near me.

I was excited because I had not seen Daddy since he left us for Mrs. Ellen and her children. He came to Texas and picked up Carl, our baby sister Liz, and me, and drove us back with him to Tulsa. Daddy had a 3-bedroom house; appropriate since he was a man.

Daddy grew marijuana in his backyard. He allowed Carl to smoke as much as he wanted, only at the house, though. He also allowed me to drink if I was at the house.

I decided to try marijuana. I walked down to the train track by Daddy's house and rolled up the marijuana joint the best I could. The joint was super big because I had never done this before. I smoked that joint and got high from two puffs.

As a result, I was seeing more than one train coming up the track. What I saw caused me to try to get off the train track. Thank God my brother came looking for me! He found me in time to get me of the track. I never touched marijuana again!

Daddy decided to take Carl and me to a club; Liz was too young. I was able to pass as an older woman. They weren't going to let Carl come in. Somehow, Daddy convinced them to let Carl in the club, though.

This was my first time in a club setting. I had two drinks: a Salty Dog and a Bloody Mary. I was drunk after just those two drinks, but I was with Daddy. We had a good time at the club. Daddy informed me that he would allow me to drink if I did the drinking at home. That was fine by me.

One day when Daddy was at work, Mrs. Ellen's daughter, Danny, suddenly came into Daddy's house with her own set of keys. Danny and I were the same age. Mrs. Ellen's children and my siblings and I had grown up together.

I asked Danny, "Who gave you keys to Daddy's house?"

With this incident, we discovered that Mrs. Ellen and Daddy were no longer together. Now he was with Danny, her daughter, who was my age: 16. Danny tried to act like she was our mother.

I blasted her out and told her, "You may be going with our Daddy, but you won't be telling us what to do."

While we were there in Oklahoma with Daddy, he was not aware I had been calling Maryann long distance on his phone. I missed Maryann so much; I wanted to be back home.

Summer ended. Daddy took Carl, Liz, and I out for burgers. He informed us that Carl and I were not going back to Texas, only Liz, our little sister.

I knew not to act out my anger because Daddy would beat me. I knew I had to do something. I made up my mind that no one was going to separate Maryann and me.

I called Mama and told her that Mrs. Ellen and Daddy were no longer together; he was now with Danny. Mama became so angry! She called Daddy and told him to bring **all** her children home. I am so glad Daddy did not think to ask how she came about that news.

Daddy brought us home one week before school started. Daddy and Mama talked to me. They told me that they did not want me hanging around Maryann's house or communicating with her. When Daddy left, Mama didn't know I met up with Maryann the very same day. We resumed our relationship.

I was so glad Daddy brought us home when he did. He received his phone bill. It was $300, mostly because of the long-distance calls I had made. Daddy assured me that if I had still been in Tulsa, he would have given me a beating.

Every time I saw Lula, Maryann's sister, she told me I was going to hell. Rhonda, one of her other sisters always shook her head when she walked past us; she was disgusted with both of us.

I was always scared of being around Maryann's sisters and family. I now believe I felt more shame than fear, though. But not Maryann! She had a mental health issue. Her family was a little afraid of her because she would go off. Only Mother Jug could calm her down.

Maryann decided to get an apartment for us. Mother Jug did not want her baby girl to move out, but Maryann moved out anyway. She found an apartment for us, and things were alright for a while. Then jealousy rose. Maryann was so jealous! If she saw me talking to a girl, another woman – it did not matter - she would go off the deep end! I always had to look over my shoulder concerning Maryann.

Even though she knew we were intimate, Miss Jugg, Maryann's mother, had allowed me to live with them. It was almost as though she did not care what we were doing. She never said a word to us about me still seeing and being with Maryann in her house.

One evening during the summer, Helena, one of Maryann's older sisters, asked me to go to the revival. It started at 7:30 that night. I told her yes but asked her to let me ask my Mama. Mama said it was fine. When they brought me home, it was extremely late; everyone was asleep at my house.

During this time, I met Mrs. Goodman – Sister June - our neighbor down the street. We became friends. Sister June loved to drink so I started drinking with her: vodka and wild turkey, straight, nothing added. I would climb out of my window at night and go to Barrett Inn. Juju and I would slow drag with the men so they could buy drinks for me. Mama never knew I was leaving the house at night.

To carry on with my new drinking habit, I sometimes went to Grover Baptist Church to get money for food which I told the Pastor my family needed. I would lie to Pastor Griffin and give him a sad story about my family's need. With the money he gave to me, I could buy vodka. When he found out what I was doing, Pastor Griffin came to the house. He told Mama what I had done. Of course, that was a beatdown for me.

Throughout all the beatings and discipline, I received from Mama, a part of me hated her. I did not understand why she did not love me like she loved my siblings. Most of the time, I believe I did bad things for attention; not because I wanted to do them. It seemed like the only time Mama paid attention to me was when she had to beat me.

Chapter 7

Hell to Deal With

In 1977, I began attending Crosby High School. My name and reputation preceded me there.

The teachers had already been informed that I had a bad behavioral problem. The reason they passed me through the other grades was because the teachers did not want to deal with me another year.

In High School, I was in Special Education classes. After all the years I had already attended school, I still did not know how to do basic Math. English, Science, History, and Social Studies were easy for me because I loved reading and writing. I was also excited about being in Music class.

I had an African American music teacher, Mrs. Dare. I knew how to act in her class because she did not play! For the most part, though, I behaved because I loved singing. Mrs. Dare was off the chain! She did not allow students to come into her class looking just any kind of way; or smelling any kind of way, for that matter.

Mrs. Dare would tell you straight up, "Get out of my class and take this soap and go wash under your arms." Or, "Take this toothpaste and brush your teeth."

She would ask questions and make comments like, "Did you forget to look in the mirror and comb your hair? Get out of my class and take this comb and go comb your hair."

Mrs. Dare did that only because she wanted us to be proud African American boys and girls. She wanted us to take pride in ourselves. She did not do any of what she did to shame us. She wanted us to be the best versions of ourselves.

"No matter what other people say about you, you are bright, intelligent, beautiful, handsome young men and ladies," she would tell us.

Mrs. Dare made us pick our heads up and stop looking down at the ground.

"That is what they want you to do. But lift your heads up and know that you are somebody!"

We had many laughs in Mrs. Dare's class. We not only learned how to sing, but we also learned how to stand together as African Americans. We were taught not to turn on each other. That was something, Mrs. Dare told us, other races and nationalities wanted us to do: turn against each other.

There were a few other teachers at Crosby who showed us that we were not coming into their classes to take over. I gave them much respect.

I was so excited about being in Mrs. Dare's class. I was one of the students chosen to participate in the ensemble choir. We would go to other states and compete.

On the day we competed, I was scared when it was our turn to perform. We did not win first place that day; we came in third. Despite our loss, Mrs. Dare still showed us that she was proud of us.

She told us, "Next year!"

We all shouted with joy.

Gloria was my best friend during this time. Our friendship was different from my other friends, Babe and Carol. We all hung together throughout our three years in High School. Gloria and I, however, had a special love for each other. We wrote to each other.

We shared how much we loved each other. Many in school thought Gloria and I were in a relationship. That was not the case: we had a bond that was not normal.

I was a leader and a great influence on my *low-class friends* as they called us. Before I gave my life to Jesus, I had many friends. I was always at the head of the lunch table, telling my friends crazy things and making them laugh.

Most of the time, I believe my friends wanted to be around me because I was not scared of anyone. I was not scared of doing daring things.

In 1977, we had a talent show. I signed up to sing and wrote this song, "I'm Not for Real."

I'm not for real.

Oh, Oh, I'm not for real.

Look, I can walk, think, and talk.

I'm real.

Oh. Boys with the hair, girls go so wide,

I'll be the one who's all the fun, cause,

I'm real.

I thought I looked so good that day. I had on my long, yellow pants, yellow and black shirt, and big heel shoes. Although I did not win first place that day, I still had a good time. I was a clown that day. They booed me off the stage, but I had plenty of fun.

One day in typing class, all the other students were finished doing their work. I played around a lot because I did not understand how to do my work. After the other students finished their homework, they were allowed to talk. I had created this porn book from a tablet; everyone was looking at the tablet.

Mrs. Greg called my name and asked if I was finished with my homework.

I told her, "No," and kept talking to my friends.

She asked me again to turn around, stop talking, and do my homework. I got so mad at Mrs. Greg: I picked up the typewriter and threw it at her. She sent me to the office with a letter.

The Principal, Mr. John, asked, once again, "Miss Beaver, what have you done this time?"

I handed him the letter: I was suspended for three days. I do not recall Mama ever coming to the school for my misbehavior. The Elementary School children laughed at us because they walked us in line when we had to go into the classrooms; almost like in jail when you think about it. I spent more time in In-School Suspension (ISS) than I stayed in the classroom.

During lunch, my friends who did not like chicken fried steak gave theirs to me. I would eat about four chicken fried steaks, mashed potatoes, green beans, and wash it all down with cold chocolate milk. On burger day, I ate about three burgers because some of my friends had money and could buy their food at the snack bar.

When it was time for the pep rally, we would all meet in the gym. One of my friends would bring a desk because I knew how to beat on the desk with rhythm. Everyone would dance to the beat, shouting, "Go Beaver; Go Beaver; Goooooo!" Their chants caused me to beat that much harder and louder.

I did not like Home Economics. Unfortunately, it was the only class I could pick as a credit. I hated sewing. One day, we were making pants. Cutting out patterns was really not my thing, but I did the work to the best of my ability.

Mrs. Jane, the Home Economics teacher, asked who wanted to sign up for cosmetology. I raised my hand because I wanted to get out of sewing. Students had to pay $20 to sign up for the class. I don't know where I obtained the money, but I turned in my $20 by the due date.

When it was time for us to transfer to the cosmetology classes, Mrs. Jane told me I could not go because of my grades. I was so mad! I told her to give me my $20 back. She said there was no refund. I asked her again; she repeated the same.

I told her, "You are going to regret not giving me my money back."

We were doing a drive to help children with different diseases. I volunteered and took the can and the little stickers you give to those who donated money. I raised so much money for that fundraiser; I had to get another can for the additional money I received. When it was time to turn the money in to Mrs. Jane, I took out the money she owed me.

When I turned in the donations to her, I told her, "I took the money out that you refused to give back to me."

She became very angry with me. She was so angry with me, in fact, she called me ugly. By this time, the eyes of all my classmates were on me.

I looked at Mrs. Jane and told her, "If ugly was a crime, they would have put you in jail a long time ago."

I also told her, "I cannot see why your husband married you, because you are so ugly."

By this time, my classmates were urging me on. Mrs. Jane said she would slap my face to the ground.

I told her, "Yes, and you better make sure when I go down that I stay down. Because if I come up, I will kill you. And that's a fact."

Yes, she sent me to the office, and reported me to the Principal. I was suspended for a week.

In 1978, I was in the 11th grade. School had started, and Mama told us we would not be able to go to school that week because we did not have school clothes to start. In spite of how I acted and how much trouble I got into while in school, I loved going to school. I was very angry that I would not be able to go because I didn't have clothes to wear.

When Mama went down the street to her friend's house to drink coffee, I went into her closet and searched for something to wear to school that day. I found a lime, two-piece suit, put it on, and went to school. I thought I was looking fly that day in Mama's two-piece lime suit!

That year, we had a cool African American substitute teacher, Mrs. Black. She acted like one of us; she was so crazy. She often talked to me about me being crazy. She told me that I needed to be cool and not get in trouble all the time. I did my best to follow Mrs. Black's instructions. Sadly, though, sometimes I got so angry, I had to fight. It was a part of me I didn't know how to fix.

Mrs. Black said, "Carla Beaver would fight a signpost if it looked at her wrong."

She was probably right. Fighting was my key to survival and not letting others control me.

Mrs. Spot was my English teacher. I did not give her any trouble in her class because, from the first time I entered her classroom, she was so sweet to me. Mrs. Spot was a Christian and had such a beautiful spirit. She took special time with me on my homework.

I was good at P.E. and at different sports. Unfortunately, because of my grades and behavior, many times I could not participate in sports. So, all I could do was play sports with my friends at school.

One time, I asked Mama for some money to buy snacks at the snack bar at school. She told me she did not have any money.

With this and other instances, I always felt that Mama did not love me. I felt that she loved my siblings more than me. Mama often told me that Carl and I were her worst children because we were always doing something to get into trouble.

Because Daddy never looked back when he left us, I became very angry with him. That anger affected everything I did. We didn't hear from him, nor did he try to provide for our needs. I felt abandoned and rejected causing emotional problems to creep up on me.

I recall Mama coming to the school one time, though. She came to the school because I had stolen some of her food stamps. I stole the food stamps and used them because I wanted to buy candy and snacks like my friends. They were able to buy snacks at the snack bar at school; I wanted to do the same.

Mama asked my brother Bob's girlfriend if I had money at school. She told Mama that I had a lot of candy, and I was passing it out to my friends. When Mama came to the school, she went to my locker to see what was in it.

Although I laughed at Mama making a fool of herself, I was smart enough to not let Mama get close enough to me to beat me in front of my classmates. All my friends and other students laughed at Mama and me, but I didn't want them to see her beating me.

During the month of February, different movies about slavery were being shown. To be honest, it seemed like these types of movies did not help African American people. If anything, these movies did more damage than good.

Tension rose in our community; also, in me. I saw the abuse our people had to go through because of the color of our skin; even the grownups.

In school, we talked about slavery. A female, Caucasian classmate looked at me during the class we were in. There was something in her look that made me go over to her.

I asked her what she was looking at. Before she could really give me an answer, I took the belt from around my waist and started beating her. The more I thought about those movies and the things my people had experienced, the harder I beat her. The harder I beat her, the longer I beat her. The longer I beat her, the more I wanted to beat her.

She was bleeding badly. Some of my classmates saw that I was very serious about beating this girl.

They were telling me, "Beaver, stop. She is bleeding."

I just kept on beating this poor girl until someone ran to the office to get help.

My friend, Gloria, was finally able to stop me. I was soaking wet from the exertion of beating this girl. I was so angry; I lost control. Only by the grace of God was I not charged for beating that girl the way I had beat her. I was suspended for next week.

Mama did not come to the school when this happened. I do not know if the school sent Mama a letter concerning my suspension or not. She never mentioned anything about the incident. When I was suspended, I did not care. After that, I felt that no one else cared what happened to me. I stopped caring for myself as well.

Chapter 8

Get Out!

It was late when I came home from the revival that night. It was 1979.

Imagine looking all around yourself in the room you call your own, and there are no walls; just the frame of the room you live in. You can see the hidden dark spiders and webs. You have no door because Daddy tried to build your house by himself and did not complete what he had started.

A Bible sat on my nightstand, full of dust because I seldom read it. I sat on the edge of my bed. I heard a soft voice call my name, *"Carla."*

I ran downstairs. I thought it was Mama trying to see if I was home. Her door was closed. I went back upstairs and sat back down on the edge of my bed. I looked at the big spiders in the dark.

The voice softly called my name again. *"Carla..."*

This time, I thought one of my brothers was trying to scare me. I went downstairs again. I stood at their bedroom door for a long time to see if I could catch one of them trying to scare me. We still only had two bedrooms downstairs. Nothing had changed about the house except for me making that space my own.

Everyone was asleep; no one moved. I stood there for a long time before going back upstairs. I kept the light on all night because I feared the spiders. As long as the lights were on, I felt they would not come and bite me. I sat back on the edge of the bed and grabbed that old dusty Bible.

For the third time, I heard the voice.

"***Carla***..."

I knew it was the Voice of God. How? I do not know. I fell to my knees; tears rolling down my cheeks.

God said, "Come unto Me and I will give you rest."

I began telling God how sorry I was for all the bad things I had been doing. I asked Him to forgive me for all my sins.

"I believe that You died and rose again."

That night, my life changed. The next night, I went back to the revival. Oh, what joy I felt inside! It was very late when the service finally ended.

Helen told me, "Just come stay with us, and you can go home in the morning."

By this time, Mama had married Mr. George. He didn't like my siblings and me very much. He was so mean to us. Everyone called him, 'Dully.'

When Dully saw me coming into the yard, he asked, "Where are you going? You do not live here anymore." He was outside rubbing on his car as usual.

I just kept walking; he followed me into the house.

He asked again, "Where are you going?"

I told him, "Into the house to get ready for school."

He followed me inside. Mama was already waiting for me. She asked where I had been. I tried to explain my story: I thought she would be happy I had given my life to Jesus.

Mama asked why I had not come home the night before. I tried to explain to her where I had been and why I had not come home the previous night. She did not want to hear what I had to say. I was a changed person, but she could not see anything because of Dully.

Mama took out the belt. For the first time, I did not run. She beat me. Tears rolled down my face. Although a part of me was hurt and sad, I felt joy also.

The only words I heard coming out of Mama's mouth were, "Get Out!"

Dully got his wish. Tears streamed down my face as I walked toward the front door with only the clothes on my back. I never looked back from that day.

By this time, my two oldest sisters, Brenda and Esther, my oldest brother Bob, and my twin, Carl, were either on the streets or in prison. My siblings were out of Mama's house. I guessed it was time for me to be out of her house as well.

I walked down St. Charles Street. On Melvin Street, the only place I felt I could go was to the Bellow's house.

A part of me was so hurt by how Mama had treated me. Throughout the years, the hurt had built up. I did not know what to do with the hurt. I did not recognize the fact that the hurt was causing me to go down a path I did not want to go down.

I walked down the street, pouring my heart out to Jesus, "Why is all this happening to me?"

I made it to the Bellow house. They were all on the porch. I was still crying when I got to Minister Helena. I laid my head on her shoulder. Crying, I told her what had happened.

"Mama told me to get out, and Mr. George said that I did not live there anymore."

Helena was the oldest saved Christian in the Bellow's home. Yet, she was unaware that it would not be a good decision for me to move in with them. The whole family already knew that Maryann and I had engaged in lesbian activity. Living with them for any amount of time would not be a good idea.

The Word of God is true.

My people are destroyed for lack of knowledge: because thou hast rejected knowledge, I will also reject thee, that thou shalt be no priest to me: seeing thou hast forgotten the law of thy God, I will also forget thy children. (**Hosea 4:6 KJV**)

The Word of God means the same as it reads: ignorance, or lack of knowledge, is one such destructive state. Ignorance can destroy just like cancer. I was in the land of lack of knowledge because I didn't know that I was living a very destructive lifestyle. There was more about my situation that I didn't know than that I did know.

Many lives have been lost; many cruel deeds have been done; many souls have perished as a result of lack of knowledge. God never wanted it to be so. That is why He gave His Word. He gave His Word so that we could seek His face to get understanding from His Word.

This was the case with the Bellow family and me. For almost all of their lives, the Bellow family had been members of Anglo Missionary Baptist Church, even before I became a member. Anglo Missionary Baptist Church was under the leadership of Pastor Keith Brown.

I was a member for a few months before Helena told Pastor Brown that Mama had put me out. Pastor Brown, with the approval of the Deacons, decided to give a love offering every month to the Bellow family to help meet my needs.

Even though I had accepted Christ into my life, I thought that this problem with Maryann and our alternative lifestyle would go away. I had a rude awakening! Giving my life to Jesus Christ did not make the problem go away. Sadly, at the time, that was what I believed. Again, lack of knowledge.

Maryann was a few years older than me. She wasn't a Christian at the time. I did not know how God felt in the Bible about two women being together, but I knew something about this was wrong. I didn't want to be with another female even though I was playing the role and agreeing to the relationship.

Even though she was older than me, Maryann still lived in the home with her mother. Late in the midnight hour when everyone was asleep in the house, I would go outside in the ditch and cry. While I was crying, I begged Jesus to take this disease away from me. I asked Him to give it to someone else; I did not want this in my life.

The Bellows knew Maryann and I were engaging in this lifestyle. They were either praying for us to get delivered or they just ignored the fact that it was still going on. Obviously, their prayers would not work if they were praying for deliverance for us both. Mostly, I felt they were ignoring what was going on with us.

In 1979, on a Saturday night, I went to a revival at St. Peter Church of God in Christ under the leadership of Pastor Jason Williams. The people were dancing and shouting. At the time, I didn't know anything about the baptism of the Holy Ghost with the evidence of speaking in other tongues. When I left that revival, I wanted to dance like they were dancing. I also wanted the Baptism of the Holy Ghost.

That Sunday, I went to my church. I had a very close relationship with Pastor Keith Brown and his wife, Carol. After church, I knocked on the Pastor's office door. He told me to come in. I told him I would like to talk to him about something that was troubling me. I shut the door and sat on one of the chairs.

I said, "Pastor Brown, I went to St. Peter Church of God in Christ's revival last night, and they were dancing and shouting and speaking in a language." I said, "Pastor, why don't we do that here?"

He said, "You must meet the qualifications."

I said, "So, they meet them, but we don't?"

He brushed this off with something else.

When I left Pastor's office, I was not happy. I decided to go on a three day and night fast. I wanted the Holy Ghost dance and the Baptism of the Holy Ghost with the evidence of speaking in other tongues. I stayed in prayer and in the Word of God for those three days. I asked God to fill me with the Holy Ghost with evidence of speaking in other tongues.

On Friday night, October 23, 1979, I was putting on a program. I had invited a Holiness church to come and be on the program. The people wanted me to cancel the service due to weather conditions. I decided to not cancel the service. Those who wanted to come could come; those who chose not to come, that would be fine.

There were a handful of those who chose to come to that Friday night service. The Holiness church people began to sing under the power of the Holy Ghost. I was in great expectation that God was going to grant my request that night.

Those sisters tarried with me until the tongues finally came up out of my belly. I had never felt the presence of God like I felt it that night. I began to praise God from my very soul. I could feel the power of the Holy Ghost burning inside of me. I began to speak in another language.

I couldn't stop! I had never been that high in the Holy Ghost in my life like that night of the service.

The only way I could explain what happened that night was in this way: it was like my heart was burning, like I was being branded in my heart with fire. I will never forget that night when the Father filled me with the Holy Ghost in Jesus' name. The fire in my heart stayed with me for weeks.

The Bellows family would have church services in their home. When they did, the power of the Holy Ghost would come into the service very heavily. I cried and shouted during these services because I wanted what was going on with Maryann and me to stop.

As I shared earlier, Maryann was becoming extremely jealous in our relationship. Whenever she thought I was looking at or talking to another woman, she became violent. One day, she hit me in the head with a cast iron skillet; she thought I was trying to talk to another female.

At one point, she threw a firecracker into my breast. The firecracker blew up. I still have the scar from that firecracker.

Pastor Brown did not know that I was struggling with the lesbian lifestyle. Highly active in the ministry, I sang in the local choir as well as the district choir. I was also a children's Sunday School Teacher. I served on the Young People's Usher Board; I was the Young Women's Auxiliary President; I organized programs for young people; I formed a drill team. I was also a missionary speaker. I was very active within the church but was still struggling with my alternative lifestyle.

Every year, we helped raise money to go to the National Baptist Convention of America. The church would pay the remainder of what we did not raise,.

To speak at the National Baptist Convention of America, you usually had to submit a form at the beginning of the year. I do not know what Pastor Brown did to convince them to let me speak that day, but that was the greatest day of my life.

The power of the Holy Ghost came all over me. I preached until the people stood up all over the building. I take no credit for what God did that day through me. All glory belongs to Him.

When I came down from the podium, I could see how proud Pastor Brown and his wife were of me. I could feel it in their hugs. It gave me a good feeling that God had used me for His glory.

Afterward, people from everywhere wanted me to come and speak to their youth. The Spirit of the Lord had me to say that I was not ready. I did not know why I said that because I felt I could do the job. But I was also still struggling with the lesbian lifestyle.

I had to go back home and deal with this problem that seemed to not want to go away. I never thought I would be free. Every time I told myself I was not going to engage in this lifestyle anymore, I yielded to it time and time again.

Even though in my heart I wanted to live right, I lived a defeated life daily. No one at the time could help me get free. Because I wanted to be free, though, I did not mind asking for help.

Sister Neal Tanner and Sister Linda Braxton were also members of Anglo Missionary Baptist Church. There were some rumors going around that they were lesbians. I don't know why, but I decided to talk to Sister Tanner about what I was dealing with. I needed some direction so I would know which way to go and what to do to get out of this trap I was currently in.

Sister Tanner talked with Pastor Brown, Sister Carol, and Sister Margaret Rose about my problem. They all decided I needed counseling. Sister Neal and Sister Joy paid for my counseling. Sister Tanner researched for a counselor. She finally found a counselor for me in downtown Houston at the Medical Center.

The meeting was scheduled for Monday morning. We all met with the counselor, Mrs. Curly Tyler. I was asked to sit in a chair outside of the room while they all went in to talk. After about 45 minutes, the door opened. Mrs. Tyler asked me to come into the room.

I went into the room. Mrs. Tyler led me to a chair in front of the room. Pastor Brown, Sister Brown, Sister Margaret Rose, and Sister Tanner all faced me. I was very nervous because I did not know what to expect.

Everyone assured me that I was not crazy; I just needed some help. Mrs. Tyler asked if I understood why I was there. I told her yes and no.

Mrs. Tyler told me that everyone felt that I needed more help than the church could give to me. She informed me I would be coming to see her twice a week.

I told Mrs. Tyler that I knew I was not crazy. Even though they all reassured me that I was not crazy, they assured me that talking things out would help me find out where I went wrong. Mrs. Tyler said that Mrs. Tanner would be bringing me on Monday and Wednesday evenings at 6 PM after I got out of school.

Pastor Keith and Mrs. Brown, and the church secretary, Miss Rose, always showed me such love. I felt that all was going to be alright.

When the sessions began, Miss Tanner picked me up at 4 PM and took me downtown. My sessions with Mrs. Tyler lasted about 45 minutes. Miss Tanner waited outside the room while I was inside for my counseling session with Mrs. Tyler. I did not tell anyone that I thought that this was stupid.

Mrs. Tyler would ask me dumb questions like, "Did you talk to a boy today?"

As time went on, I began telling her what she wanted to hear, even though none of those things were happening in my life.

For two months, Miss Tanner came and picked me up on Mondays and Wednesdays for my counseling sessions. One Wednesday at 4 PM when Miss Tanner picked me up, all was well until she asked if I had met a young man that day.

I answered her question truthfully; I could tell she did not believe me. I always told the truth about myself: good or bad. I was like that because I wanted to really do what was right.

Miss Tanner said, "You better not be lying to me."

I told her, "No, Ma'am. I am telling you the truth."

I became terribly angry and became noticeably quiet. I would not say anything.

Miss Tanner got mad with me because I did not say a word for the remainder of the ride home. We made it to my address. With an angry tone, Miss Tanner told me she would no longer be taking me to the counseling sessions.

I was glad that all this going to a counselor to talk about if I met a young man was over. I was angry with Miss Tanner because she did not believe I was telling the truth. I had a problem when I told the truth and someone did not believe me. I did not like it when people thought I was lying and I was telling the truth.

Maryann and I worked at Blue Hill Nursing Home in Baytown, Texas. It was extremely challenging working on the same job as her. If she saw me or thought I was talking to another female, she would grab me. I would have to run and hide for a while so she could not find me.

We moved into an apartment together. I guess she was tired of her family telling us we were going to hell. During this time, Maryann also had relationships with men. I believe she did that to mess up my mind. Believe me, it worked. She was very possessive and didn't want me to talk to other females.

In 1984, I moved back in with Miss Belinda Tate Jackson who was an RN. I stayed with her for a while just to get away from all the mental and physical abuse I was experiencing with Maryann. Our relationship finally came to an end. I was so glad to get out from under the fear, and the mental and physical abuse.

I became friends with Joe. He and I attended the same ministry. Brother Joe was interested in me, but I didn't know that at the time. I had never had a relationship with a male before.

I loved playing Pac-Man. I repeatedly played that game. Brother Joe would come to the house during his lunch break from his job and eat lunch with me.

One day when he came at noon, he handed me a box wrapped in beautiful wrapping paper. I was excited because I love surprise gifts. I tore the wrapping paper off. To my surprise, it was my own Pac-Man game.

I gave Joe a hug and thanked him. We sat down on the floor, ate, and played Pac-Man until it was time for him to go back to work. I was still unaware that this young brother was interested in me. There is one event I will never forget, though.

We went to the mall one Saturday evening. We went to the jewelry store and looked at different jewelry. He asked if I liked some diamond earrings he was pointing out to me.

I told him, "Yes. They are so beautiful."

He called the clerk and told him we wanted to purchase those earrings. The earrings were over $300! Joe paid cash. I felt so special. No man had ever bought anything for me, especially something so expensive.

Joe took the earrings out of the box and put them in my ears. I had to hold back the tears. I was so excited! I told Joe to drop me at Diana's house so I could show off my earrings. We drove into Diana's driveway; I couldn't wait to get out of the car. I felt like a little girl.

We knocked on the door. Diana said, "Come in."

Joe and I entered her house.

I was so hyped up, Diana asked, "What is wrong with you?"

I pointed to my ears.

She said, "Wow!"

I told her, "Brother Joe bought them for me."

I didn't tell her that he had told me that the next piece of jewelry he would buy for me would be a ring.

After Brother Joe left, Diana said, "Carla, that brother likes you. Can't you see that?"

I said, "No."

Diana looked me straight in my face and said, "No man goes around buying expensive diamond earrings for a woman unless he is interested in her."

Then I told her, "He said next time it's going to be a diamond ring."

Diana said, "He bought you the Pac-Man game that you love to play. Then he turns around and buys you expensive diamond earrings. And next he wants to give you a ring? Girl, open your eyes! This man cares about you!"

One evening, Brother Joe took me to his apartment. He showed me some of his pictures as we drank lemonade. There was one picture I believe he really wanted me to see. He looked like a bodybuilder in the picture; he was so fine. A part of me wanted to ask him what had happened. I decided that this would not be very nice.

I was feeling something I had never felt before. Although I couldn't put a name to it, it made me feel good inside.

One day, I was at home waiting for our normal routine. Noon came; Brother Joe never showed up that day. I called Diana to tell her that Brother Joe did not come to eat his lunch with me that day. She suggested that maybe he had to work through his lunch break that day.

"I'm sure you will hear from him today with an explanation."

I never received a call from him that day. I called him but he never answered my calls. Tuesday came; I still didn't hear from Brother Joe. I felt that something was wrong; I just didn't know what had happened.

I called Diana to tell her I still had not seen or heard from Brother Joe for two days.

"Maybe I will see him tomorrow at Bible Study," I said to her.

She said, "You probably will, and I am sure he had a good reason that you have not seen or heard from him."

Wednesday, I went to Bible Study as usual. There was Brother Joe. But he acted very strangely toward me. He spoke to me, but I felt a distance between us.

After Bible Study, I thought for sure Brother Joe would come over and we would talk like we always did. That didn't happen.

He said, "Goodnight," and left.

I asked Sister Barbara to tell Diana to call me as soon as she could.

Diana called. She asked, "Did Brother Joe explain why he has not talked to you or come by your house for three days?"

I told her, "No, but something has changed between Brother Joe and me. I felt such a distance between us. He was not ugly or mean; but it was like he didn't want to be in my presence."

I cried on the phone with Diana.

I asked her, "What have I done wrong? Why is Brother Joe acting the way he is acting?"

I was very hurt by Brother Joe's actions. Although he spoke to me when he came into my presence, he stopped coming by the house to eat lunch and play Pac-Man with me. At the time, I didn't know the reason why. In the Baptist church I was attending, they didn't teach on the spirit of rejection. I didn't know that's what I felt inside.

Some years went by. I found out why Brother Joe had stopped coming around me and lost interest in me. Someone had told him I was a lesbian. When I heard the reason, I cried that entire week. I didn't want to talk to anyone, not even Diana. The hurt was so deep.

Once again someone rejected me; all because of my past. At the time, I wasn't engaging in a female or lesbian relationship.

I felt that part of my life was over. Now in a new phase, I thought I was going to maybe get married and have a family of my own. I decided to move out of Mrs. Jackson's home because we were going to different ministries and didn't believe in the same things.

Sister Barbara Rose, the secretary of the church, took me in with her family. Everything was going great. Diana Rose was the Anglo Missionary Baptist Church musician for the Male choir, youth, and senior choirs. Diana would use her own money to purchase the choir music for the church. She worked on the choir songs late into the night for choir rehearsal. I was one of the main lead singers. Diana did not play with you when it came down to perfecting those songs.

One day I decided to share with Diana the things I had been dealing with since I was 17. Diana never treated me any differently after I told her about Maryann. Diana went on like nothing had changed.

When we had night service, Diana didn't attend those services. She would drop her mother, Mrs. Barbara Rose, and me at the house of God, and she would go about her business.

I soon discovered that Diana wasn't quite delivered at the time. Many times, when she dropped her mother and me at the night service, I asked her if she was staying.

Diana would tell me, "No."

When I asked her why, she would always say, "I am going to have sex."

I always told her I was going to tell Pastor Brown. She would laugh and drive out of the parking lot, leaving me standing there shaking my head.

I had no doubt that Diana Rose loved me as a sister and friend. Diana was a true friend to me. I could trust her with my life. I felt very safe being in Diana's home.

Sister Barbara Rose is the sweetest Woman of God you will ever meet. She always had a smile on her face. I never heard her complain about anything. When Sister Barbara entered the room, she lit up the room with that smile.

I had to sleep in the same bed as Sister Barbara because she only had a four-bedroom house. Diana, her brother, Mark, and Diana's son, Steve, all had their own rooms. I didn't mind because Sister Barbara treated me like I was her daughter. I felt such love from her; the love I had wanted to feel from my own mother.

Diana was very committed to the ministry of music. She loved what she was doing in ministry. We formed a group: True Victory. That was our theme song: True Victory. There were seven of us in the group from the choir: John, Danny, Paul, Carol, Paula, Task, and me. Diana was our musician.

We sang at different church programs; we even sang in Houston. After we got out of service, we always went to Pizza Hut and laughed and talked through the morning. We were the older ones that were in the Anglo Missionary Baptist Church Youth Choir. We would practice at Sister Diana's house. Afterward, we would either go out to eat, or Sister Barbara Rose would cook for us. We had so much fun. We were all committed to our singing ministry.

I know this sounds strange, but I never let another female make love to me. I was the one that gave love. I never allowed them to return that love to me. I only accepted the things they gave me as a token of their love for me. I didn't have to worry about my car being fixed. Ruth made sure I had whatever I needed.

In 1986, I met Ruth Belfort. Ruth was an older woman who grew up in Anglo Missionary Baptist Church with her parents. Ruth had left the church. When I became a member, she was not attending church. Ruth returned to Anglo.

I don't recall how Ruth and I became friends. We began by just talking. Then, she would buy whatever I wanted or needed: clothes, shoes, car, etc. She began showing me so much attention; I fell right into the trap again.

I ended up moving out of Diana Rose's house into an apartment with Ruth. Diana begged me to not do that because everyone at the church knew what lifestyle Ruth lived.

All those years I was a member of Anglo, neither my leaders nor those who knew my struggle ever pointed out to me in the Word of God concerning how God felt about my lifestyle. The people I lived with who were having church services and casting out demons in their homes never took me to the Word of God.

I was never counseled by any of those who condemned me. All they could tell me was, "You are going to hell."

Ruth sometimes went out with her boyfriend and stayed out late. When she did that, I would go to the adult video place and rent at least 10 xxx rated videos of women having sex with men and watch them all night. I convinced myself that I needed to watch those xxx rated videos so that when I did get married, I would know how to make love with my husband.

I also began to masturbate until I reached a climax. I would get so angry because the climax did not last long, and I could not keep going. I would get mad because Ruth was also out with a man. It never dawned on me that something was wrong with this entire situation I was living in.

I believe Ruth was getting tired of me. Every time I made love to her, afterward, I would cry so hard all night, repenting to God because I really did not want to do what I was doing. The relationship I had with women was always one-sided. I did not want anyone to touch me in an improper way. Even with that, I should have known that something was not quite right with how I was allowing myself to be treated.

As I mentioned earlier, Ruth also had men in her life. If you could only imagine the mental stress and fear cluttering my mind! Sometimes when she left me alone some nights to spend time with her men friends, I trembled in fear, jealous I was going to lose the one that had shown me love and acceptance.

Our relationship deteriorated. Ruth became very tired of all the crying I was doing after I sinned.

Many of you would have counted me out a long time ago. But there was a calling on my life and I knew it.

Satan also knew there was a calling on my life. He did everything he could to kill my desire to serve the Lord. He stole my joy and peace and attempted to destroy me in the process. Maybe I did or maybe I didn't have to go through all I went through to be free; I won't know until I appear before the Lord. But God saw my heart throughout it all. That's all that mattered.

It is true what the Word of God says...

But the Lord said to Samuel, *"Do not consider his appearance or his height, for I have rejected him. The Lord does not look at the things people look at. People look at the outward appearance, but the Lord looks at the heart."* (**1 Samuel 16:7 NIV**)

After Saul disobeyed God's command, God sent Samuel the Prophet to anoint David to be a *king after God's own heart.* (**1 Samuel 13:14**)

Even though Samuel was a spiritual man, he, too, was guilty of looking at the outer appearance of David's older brothers. Samuel looked at their height; how big their muscles were; how stern they were; and whether they had a *kingly* presence. Yet, God rejected every one of David's brothers that were presented to Samuel.

David's own father didn't even consider David to be the choice God would have made. In God's rejection of all of David's brothers, God made known the difference between Himself and the world when it comes to judging people. We look at how a person looks on the outside, never judging the **heart** of a person. God's choice was the youngest – David - the one who was tending sheep.

We often spend so much time, money, and energy to look a certain way. Therefore, Satan deceives us by appearances. It is natural for us to be this way, but God's ways are not our ways. Even scripture indicates that Jesus had no beauty or majesty to attract us to Him, nothing in His looks that we would even desire Him.

He was despised and rejected by mankind, a man of suffering, and familiar with pain. Like one from who people hide their faces he was despised, and we held him in low esteem. (**Isaiah 53: 3 NIV**)

Outward looks can sometimes reflect an inward state of character. But it is all too easy to be deceived. Satan was the most beautiful of all created angelic beings, but his heart was ugly.

I know with everything in me that God saw my heart. He saw the many tears I shed because I wanted to be free. I did not want the things occurring in my life to be all there was about me. I wanted more. I believed that God had something more for me.

Many things I went through were some of my own choosing because of disobedience and unbelief. I was sort of like the Children of Israel. What would have been an 11-day journey took them 40 years of wandering in the wilderness until all the old had died...because of their disobedience and unbelief. (**See Exodus 3:8**)

Chapter 9

Running for My Life

In 1981, I started connecting with and talking to Brother David Jock. He was a Gospel DJ on 90.9 FM radio station in Houston. I guess I just needed someone to talk to about my problems. After a few months of talking with Brother Jock, he told me to share what I was going through with Miss Eileen.

Brother Jock told me that Miss Eileen was a very nice, Christian Woman of God. He asked if I would like to come to Spring, Texas and meet Miss Eileen.

I told him, "YES!"

I told Mama Bellow that I was leaving Saturday morning and moving to Spring. She tried to convince me to stay, but I left anyway.

I packed everything I had at the Bellow house. When the phone rang, I knew it was Brother David calling to tell me he was outside. I was right; he was outside. Although I was a little bit scared leaving familiar ground, I felt that I had to get out of this craziness!

I was shocked when Brother David got out of the car. I was looking for this tall, handsome man that matched the voice I had been listening to for months. Brother David was short, dark, and had a stomach. But he had been very nice on the phone. Even though he was no Billy Dee Williams, he was just as nice in person.

We talked all the way to Spring, Texas. When we arrived at Miss Eileen's apartment, he helped me bring my things in. We said our goodbyes.

When I knocked on her door, Miss Eileen said, "Who is it?"

I said, "Sister Carla."

When she opened the door, she was already in her nightclothes. She invited me in and told me to make myself at home. Once I got settled, Miss Eileen went back upstairs to bed. She left me downstairs alone.

I thought to myself, "Carla, what have you gotten yourself into now?"

I thought it was strange that Miss Eileen just left me downstairs by myself. I sat on the sofa and looked all around her apartment. A few hours passed; Miss Eileen came down the stairs. She asked if I was hungry. I told her that I was. She said we were going to get something to eat as soon as she got dressed.

Miss Eileen went back upstairs to get dressed. I waited another hour. She came down and told me that after we ate, she had to go to her sister's house to pick up her children.

I was a little quiet when Miss Eileen told me that Brother David had told her my story. She told me she knew a lady named Miss Dear who housed young ladies who had been in jail. I didn't know if I should be alarmed about this; I had not been in jail. She said she was sure Miss Dear had room for me to stay with her and the ladies in her care.

In my mind, all I knew was that I had been running from place to place, trying to find a place for me because I had no peace in sin.

While we were sitting eating, Miss Eileen called Miss Dear. She told her my story.

Miss Dear told Miss Eileen, "Yes. I have a room. She can help me keep the place up and clean."

For some reason, I really didn't want to go and stay with Miss Dear; I wanted to stay with Miss Eileen. I just felt more comfortable in my spirit about staying with Miss Eileen.

We arrived at Miss Dear's home. When Miss Eileen knocked on the door, a young lady opened the door. Miss Eileen told the young lady that we were there to see Miss Dear. The young lady led us to Miss Dear. Miss Eileen introduced us.

Miss Dear asked where my things were; I told her they were in Miss Eileen's car. The young lady who had let us in helped me get my things out of the car and into the house.

Miss Eileen hugged me and told me she had to go and pick up her kids. I didn't really feel right living with Miss Dear, but what could I do? I had nowhere else to go.

Very withdrawn, I stayed to myself if Miss Dear didn't have me doing things. I didn't voluntarily start conversations or try to engage with the other residents.

After living at Miss Dear's for a few months, she took us to her other home on Memorial Street. She had a big house there. Miss Dear began cutting me off from the people who loved and cared for me. I had a problem with that. She even stopped me from calling Pastor Brown and my family.

It was as though I could never be by myself to call any of my family. I didn't even know if I was ever going to see them again. Miss Dear didn't harm me, though. She just cut me off from friends and family. She isolated me.

Miss Eileen called one day when I was in the kitchen cleaning with Miss Dear. Miss Eileen must have asked how I was doing and wanted to speak to me. I had been wondering how I was going to get Miss Eileen over so she could know what was going on and get me out of this place.

I asked Miss Eileen if she would come by and see me. I told her I would love to see her again.

Miss Eileen didn't come right away. A few days after our conversation, though, there was a knock on the door. It was Miss Eileen! I was so happy to see her!

She could see that something was going on. She asked Miss Dear if she could take me to get something to eat. Miss Dear said that would be fine.

As soon as we got into Miss Eileen's car and she drove away from Miss Dear's house, I started crying. She asked what was wrong. I told her I didn't want to go back and stay with Miss Dear any longer. I asked Miss Eileen if I could use her phone to call my Pastor. She gave the phone to me.

I called Pastor Keith Brown: he was so glad to hear from me. He told me that everyone was worried because they had not heard from me in months. I told him that Miss Dear would not let me call them, and I thought I would never see them again.

In 1981, I moved back with Miss Eileen to Spring, Texas with her two children, six-year-old Kalie, and four-year-old April. At the time, she worked for Christian Radio Station KLBJ FM in Humble, Texas. After she spoke with Pastor Brown, Miss Eileen assured him that I could live with them. She never took me back to Miss Dear's house. Because I had left all my possessions at Miss Dear's, all I had were the clothes on my back.

Miss Eileen soon became a big sister to me. Although she was hard around the edges, she was such a beautiful woman inside. I knew she cared about me as time went by.

Because she worked for a Christian Radio Station, many times she was called upon to be the Mistress of Ceremony for various church programs. Miss Eileen took me along with her to those services.

After the services, I would get the keys from Miss Eileen and sit in the car until she finished fellowshipping with the people.

One night when she got in the car after spending time with the people, she told me, "From now on, you are going to start interacting with the people after the services."

No longer would I be allowed to withdraw in my shell and not talk to people. Interacting with others was very hard for me. I did not feel good about myself; I felt that I was not good enough; I didn't think I was smart enough or beautiful enough, so, I withdrew into my own world.

Kalie and April and I became very close. It felt so good taking care of them. They looked up to their big sister...me.

Miss Eileen also told me that I had "better get in that car and start driving."

One day, I got into the car and did just that. Of course, I was scared; I had never driven a car before. I got in the car and backed out and started driving all over the city. I began taking Kalie and April to the park. We also went to McDonald's; they were such good kids.

One day, I received a call from Crosby, Texas from my sister. "Joel is dead," she told me.

I began crying. Miss Eileen asked what was wrong. I told her that my stepdaddy, George, had shot and killed my brother, Joel. Miss Eileen held me in her arms while I cried.

I prepared to go back to Barrett Station. This was one of the saddest moments for our family. I really thought Mama was going to lose her mind.

We all gathered in Mama's house. We had family members come from New Orleans because of my older brother's death. There was a knock at the door. When they opened the door, George, Mama's husband, stood there.

He said, "What is going on here?"

My brothers, Bob and Carl, and our Uncle Derrick ran towards the door after George. They were going to kill him. Fortunately, our other Uncle Davis was able to stop another fatality.

Growing up in Barrett Station as children, we experienced as many hurts and pain as Mama. I wondered to myself if there would be a silver lining somewhere; when will the pain ever stop?

After the funeral, I returned to Spring to Miss Eileen, Kalie, and April. At the time, Miss Eileen was attending Pastor Bob Green's church in Spring, a predominantly white church. All my life I had only attended African American churches. I felt that these white people didn't know how to praise the Lord.

I didn't want to go to this church. Living with Miss Eileen, though, I had no choice.

When we got there, I heard the people praising the Lord. We sat down. As they continued singing and praising the Lord, a sister took off and started shouting. Then, someone else did the same. I couldn't believe my eyes! They **DID** know how to praise the Lord just like us!

From that day, I saw things in a different light.

Pastor Bob preached such powerful messages under the power of the Holy Ghost. We had an awesome time with the Lord. Pastor Bob asked if anyone wanted to get baptized in Jesus' name. I felt the presence of the Lord in that place!

I ran forward, shouting, "YES!"

The next Sunday, I was baptized in the name of Jesus. I can't explain the presence of the Lord that came all over me. I shouted and praised God in those services like I had never done before in any other service. That was not all, though.

After the service, Miss. Eileen came up to me; she was not alone. There was this tall, handsome young man with her.

She came up to me and said, "Sister Carla, this is Brother Gary Jones. He is a member also and lives here in Spring."

We shook hands and started talking. Brother Jones asked if he could call me sometime. I told him that would be fine. Something about Brother Gary caused me to be comfortable with him. He would call, and we would talk for such a long time. I felt that here was someone who would finally see me as a woman.

Brother Gary made me feel something I had never felt before: special. We would meet at church and sit together during the services.

Brother Gary was a very strong Christian man. He loved God with all his heart. What he saw in me, I didn't know; but it felt good. I had always wanted a family and children of my own.

Miss Eileen was so happy for Brother Gary and me. I still had this war going on inside of me. The war was telling me that I could not defeat this thing that had bound me for so many years. At the time, I didn't believe I could ever be set free from a lesbian lifestyle. I didn't believe I could have a normal life like every other woman. I couldn't see the forest because of the trees.

Miss Eileen tried to help me see what was in front of me: a very nice young Man of God who cared about me and wanted more from and for me. He was not only saved and filled with the Holy Ghost and fire, but he also had a very nice job with an engineering company.

Brother Gary wanted to marry me. I couldn't see what he saw in me as a Woman of God. I kept thinking about what he would do if he found out I had been involved in lesbian relationships.

I felt that I wasn't good enough for him. So, I decided to go back to the hell house I came from. Brother Gary begged me to not leave Spring; Miss Eileen also asked me not to go. Unfortunately, I could not let go of the past.

Chapter 10

Gifts and Calling!

For the gifts and the calling of God are irrevocable [for He does not withdraw what He has given, nor does He change His mind about those to whom He gives His grace or to whom He sends His call.] **(Romans 11:29 AMP)**

Gifts are given by God even before we are born. Callings and gifts are inside of us; we are born with them. You need no repentance to have them or to receive them because they were given from the beginning.

We cannot judge someone by gifts on whether they are holy or filled with the Holy Spirit. Gifts can't give full evidence of the Holy Spirit in a person because they are without repentance.

Today, there are many people outside of the church who are operating in gifts. Unfortunately, many of them are heathens and not Christians. I have seen those people speaking in tongues and prophesying, but they are not born-again and have not repented. They have gifts but are not living in holiness! You see, God blesses those He chooses to bless...no matter who the person is.

There are also many gifted people who sing and preach but are still in the clubs and the disco. They are anointed with gifts of singing from God but are still serving Satan. Understand that people can still be ministering in church, even being used with gifts, while they are leading many to hell and deceiving many people.

So, let your prayers be for seeking more of the fruits of the Holy Spirit by repentance and a righteous life more so than gifts. Gifts will not allow you to enter Heaven; they are for earthly service to others. Many are still holding those gifts while not even born-again and living in a spiritual world of darkness.

In 1990, I witnessed this for myself.

Evangelist Shirley Dillard invited me to a revival they were having at their ministry. I decided to go that Friday night and drove there by myself. I had neither heard nor met Evangelist Rhonda Edwards before this time.

When I entered the service, Evangelist Rhonda was preaching, laying hands, and prophesying to the people. God was really moving in this service. At about 10 PM, the revival ended.

I was talking to some of my sisters in the ministry. My friend, Evangelist Dillard, came over with the guest evangelist and introduced us. Evangelist Rhonda and I shook hands.

Evangelist Shirley asked if she could ask me a favor. She asked if I could let Evangelist Rhonda spend the night at my apartment and then bring her with me to Houston the next morning to catch her plane at 10 AM. She told me that Evangelist Rhonda had another program she needed to get to the next day.

I told Evangelist Shirley that would be fine. We were all going out to eat that night; Evangelist Rhonda and I were in the same car. As I followed my friends, Pastor Brad and Evangelist Shirley, to the restaurant, I could feel myself being sexually drawn toward Evangelist Rhonda.

We had a good fellowship at the restaurant. We ate, talked, and laughed until it was time for us to all go to our different places. Pastor Brad put Evangelist Rhonda's luggage in my car; we all said goodbye. Evangelist Rhonda and I drove off. When we got to my apartment, I knew I was going to have to struggle through that night. I gave my room to Evangelist Rhonda; I took the couch.

I showed Evangelist Rhonda to the bathroom and gave her towels so she could shower. We both took our showers; she went to the bedroom. I fixed up the sofa for myself. As the night progressed, Evangelist Rhonda called me to come and sleep in the room. She felt bad that she had taken my bed.

I told her it was alright. Even though there was a strong drawing in my flesh, I fought to keep myself from going into that room with her. She was persistent. I finally gave in. I went into the room and got into the bed. She was a tall, beautiful woman. I wrestled with this woman and the spirits surrounding us all night.

She put her long, pretty legs over mine. I removed her legs; she put them back. She then got so close under me; I could feel the burning in my flesh. And yet, I did not want to submit to this spirit. I really wanted to do what was right at that time.

I finally got angry with myself. A part of me wanted to be with her.

I said to her, "You just got through preaching, laying hands, and prophesying to people. And you're acting like this with me?"

I struggled throughout the night until the morning with this woman. I did not have to stay in that bed, but I could not move after I went into the room.

The next morning, I got up and put my clothes on. I told her I was ready to take her to Houston to catch her plane. I made it to George Bush International Airport and made sure she was checked in. I didn't leave until she was waiting to board her plane.

I never saw Evangelist Rhonda Edwards again. I was not angry with her; I was angrier with myself. A part of me wanted to have a sexual relationship with her that night. I cried and repented to God for even wanting to have that relationship with her. I continued to live this up and down, merry-go-round lifestyle.

Many have gifts and speak in tongues but are immoral and living a sinful life. Does that mean they are not saved? No! It just means that there are areas in their lives in which they need deliverance. But to continue to sin and not seek deliverance is another story. This is not always the case in all instances.

It is good to have gifts. It is more important, though, to have the fruit of the Holy Spirit which is the evidence of God's Spirit in us.

Chapter 11

The Separation

In 1992, I knew nothing about the gifts of the Spirit or the operation of the Spirit. There was urgency in my spirit, though; I just had to tell of God's goodness.

We did not have a place in our services for me to share, to testify. So, during the time when they opened the doors of the church for those who wanted to join or to come for Water Baptism, the Deacons would set up the chairs for those who wanted to come forward. The church would sing the song, "Come to Jesus While You Have Time."

I would sometimes be the only one sitting in the chairs. Then, I would share about God's goodness. The Holy Ghost would get all over me. The things I would say did not come from me, though. At the time, I didn't even know about prophecy or prophesying. Later, as I moved to another ministry, I was taught about the Gifts of the Spirit of God.

Some of the members of the Anglo Missionary Baptist Church started getting mad at me while I was giving my testimony. I didn't know that some of the things I was saying during my testimony were about them. I was not aware of what God was saying through me at that time.

The Bellow Family would also be shouting and crying while I gave my testimony. Annette would fall on the floor under the benches.

Other members of the church would have to try to get her up off the floor.

Two years passed. I was still at Anglo Missionary Baptist Church serving with the Drill Team. I felt an urgency in my spirit to relieve myself of all the other activities I was involved in at Anglo. I only remained faithful to the Drill Team; that precious group was my heart. I held each of the children on the team near and dear to my heart.

I was out and about one day when I met up with Danny. She began to minister to me about what the Lord had told me two years before. He had told me that it was time to leave the church; I had not obeyed. Danny told me that God was going to step in if I did not obey right then.

I was a little angry with Danny after she left. I did not want to leave the Drill Team.

On another Sunday in October, I had a talk with Pastor Brown. I wondered how to explain that I sensed this urgency in my spirit that I must leave. At the time, I didn't know where I was going to go from there. I was still a baby in the Lord. I really didn't know the movement of the Holy Spirit because I hadn't been taught about that at Anglo Missionary Baptist Church.

I went into his office and sat down, tears in my eyes. I said, "Pastor Brown, the Lord is telling me that it is time for me to leave."

He said, "That is a lie. God is not telling you to leave."

Pastor Brown was very serious when he spoke those words to me. I didn't want to leave, but I felt compelled to.

My youngest sister, Liz, was attending Faith Impact Ministry in Baytown, Texas under the leadership of Pastors Marvin T. and Kathleen Boyd. Liz was so excited about the ministry. I decided to visit that Sunday morning. Sister Samsung was the Sunday School

Teacher that morning. I had never heard a woman with such fire coming from her teaching. She sounded like a preacher!

The sanctuary was packed: wall to wall. There was no extra seating in the building. Suddenly, the Holy Ghost came into that place. People began to get happy and started speaking in tongues. There was shouting all over the building. I had never witnessed a service like that in all my life. In my spirit, I knew that this was the place. By the guidance of the Holy Spirit, I knew I should join this congregation.

In my spirit, I realized that this was where God wanted me to become a member. Well, you know the devil was not going to let me off the hook that easily.

I had a little problem at my other church. I let the children pick out the candy we would sell to raise money for the Drill Team. The team was going to the National Convention of America. The candy was not for adults; so the parents were not buying the candy. Deacons Melvin Smith and Donovan Jones were involved with this event. I had always had a run in with these deacons. They thought that Pastor Keith favored me and allowed me special privileges in the church.

By this time, I had left Ruth Belfort and moved into my own apartment. She could see the change in me; it made her extremely uncomfortable.

Ruth helped me obtain furniture and whatever I needed for my apartment. Ruth could tell that our relationship was coming to an end. But a part of her was still trying to hold on to me.

I received a call on a Tuesday that I was to come and meet with Deacons Smith and Jones and Pastor Keith concerning what I was doing about the candy. Sisters Carol Brown, Margaret Rose, Helena Smith, Grace Smith, and Lula Smith also worked with the Drill Team. They came to support me.

I went to Anglo Missionary Baptist Church on the next day,

Wednesday afternoon. Deacon Smith, Deacon Jones, Pastor Brown, his wife, Sister Carol, and the other ladies were all there in the meeting.

Deacon Smith said to me, "You are trying to leave Anglo Missionary Baptist Church and leave the church with all this candy that you ordered."

Deacon Jones asked, "Who told you to order this candy?"

Mind you that the company I ordered the candy from would not have approved the order without Pastor Brown's consent.

Deacon Smith turned to Pastor Brown and asked, "Did you give Sister Carla permission to order this candy?"

Deacon Smith looked at Pastor Brown who was looking, me straight in the eye. Then he looked at Deacon Smith and said, "No, I did not give Carla permission to order this candy."

He hung his head down; he saw the tears rolling down my face. He knew he had just lied. Except for the deacons, everyone in the room knew he had lied.

I would have never believed that Pastor Brown would lie, especially with something like this. I had such respect for him as my pastor and as a father figure in my life.

My heart dropped to the floor. Another man in my life had let me down. Nothing else could have made me leave Shiloh...except my leader lying outright to my face in the presence of all those who knew he had given me permission to order the candy.

I never looked back after that day. I joined Faith Impact Ministry with Pastors Marvin T. and Kathy Boyd.

Pastor Boyd was a powerful man of God. He was also very humble. When he preached or taught, the power of the Holy Ghost would come into the place. The people of God would go up into the Spirit.

To my surprise and dismay, I was approached and hit on by several sisters in the house of God. As much as the Spirit of God was in that house, it was hard for me to believe what was happening. I never breathed a word to leadership.

One day, I was struggling with some things. I needed to talk with someone. I went to church. Lily told me to go to the sanctuary because Sister Doretta was there dealing with some problems as well. I went into the sanctuary. She was at the altar crying out to the Lord. I fell on my knees and cried out to the Lord with her. We both got released in prayer.

Sister Doretta came with me to my house. I shared with her about my lifestyle. She did not treat me any differently. I met her husband and family. They treated me like I was a part of their family.

At the time, I was over the programs of the ministry, and Sister Doretta did the programs. We worked closely together. I sometimes spent the night at her house while we were trying to get the programs together for upcoming services.

Then, I met Sister Laura. We both had cleaning service businesses. We became friends. She had a very strong lust spirit in her. I recognized it because I could feel that spirit when it was pulling on my flesh. Sister Laura and Sister Doretta both worked with me while we were putting on the special programs for the ministry. I oversaw contacting the ministers who were going to preach for those services as well as the others who were going to be involved in the programs.

When I became a member of Faith Impact Ministry, I had many encounters with women in the ministry who approached me in an unnatural way. I wondered if I had a sign on my back that indicated I was engaging in that type of lifestyle. Yet, somehow, they knew.

During that time, Sister Claudette and I became good friends. She was married and had two children. She was not satisfied with her marriage. Even though I was not physically attracted to her, the spirit that drove me to do the things I did began to play with her emotions.

She often came to my house. The lust demon would seduce her until she didn't know what she was feeling. Finally, I began to engage in a sexual way with Sister Claudette; she turned me off. She ran to the closet in shame. That lust demon just looked at her and laughed.

We never engaged in that activity again, but we remained friends. Many times, when I saw attractive women, that lust demon tried to seduce them into a lesbian relationship with me.

Oftentimes, I could recognize that it was not really me enforcing that type of behavior. I realized that it was a driving force behind what I was doing. Because I always felt defeated, I never tried hard to fight the feeling. It was a very strong, controlling spirit.

I began masturbating. I would masturbate until I reached a climax. Afterward, I would get so angry with myself because the climax didn't last long. I attempted the process again within that same timeframe until the bed was soaking wet. I was trying to get that feeling again, but it did not happen in that timeframe.

One day, Sister Laura came over. My leaders were out of town. We found ourselves in a compromising position. This sister was expecting me to do something I was neither willing nor ready to do at the time. After that incident, we never did that again.

I got so tired of repenting over the same thing. I went to the store and purchased some liquor with which I took pain pills. I just wanted to end my life. Sister Boyd was so concerned about me. I had talked to her earlier and I wasn't in a good state of mind.

Sister Boyd kept calling me; I would not answer the phone. She then called Sister Doretta. They finally called the police. I heard knocking on the door, but I was extremely drunk. I struggled to get to the door to see who was knocking.

I finally made my way to the door. When I opened the door, the policeman asked if I was OK.

I said, "Yes, Sir."

I can't even explain how I pulled that off. He told me to call my family, then left.

In Faith Impact Ministry, we had many great services. I gave Sister Doretta and Sister Laura the rough draft, and they would do whatever else the program needed. I was living with my leaders and their four boys. I was taking care of the boys and their home.

Pastor Boyd began Faith Impact Ministry with a big group. Many of them left because they did not want him to evangelize; just pastor the church. Those that stayed had a deep love for Pastor and Sister Boyd. Everything we put together for them was done in such love, even the guests marveled.

We once had an Evangelist come to town who was only supposed to be there for one night. By God's divine will, that night turned into a week. The power of the Holy Ghost was so heavy in that place! Even without any advertisement, people came to the services by word of mouth!

The place was packed every night. The anointing in those services made demons uncomfortable. They manifested during the services.

I will never forget that Sunday morning service. Evangelist Joe Hubbard began to preach. He was under such a heavy anointing; he had to be carried out of the sanctuary.

When Pastor Boyd stood up, he was also high in the Holy Ghost. Demons began to scream and walk the benches. The delivery team began to take attendees out into the rooms and cast demons out of them.

During our Wednesday Night Bible Study, Pastor Boyd told us to write down anything we felt we were dealing with that was outside of the normal. That was when I shared with them about the lesbian lifestyle I had struggled with for most of my life.

They told me to write down everything I could think of no matter what it was. They told me they were going to do deliverance with me. They were going to give themselves over to fasting and praying, and they would let me know. At that time, I was dealing with Sister Laura. Her problem was not that she was a lesbian; she had a strong lust demon.

Lust does not care how it gets satisfied. It just wants to be satisfied. When my leaders were gone from their house, Sister Laura would come over as I shared earlier. I believe she was expecting something else; she was not satisfied with me making love to her.

We never got together again in that way. We stayed friends. I had already promised my Pastor that I didn't want to be anything like that anymore. This Sister was expecting me to do something I was not ready to do.

Sister Doretta and I were friends for a long time. I shared my past with her. I trusted she would keep it to herself, and she did.

One day, I was in the beauty shop talking to my friend, Sister Becky Curtis. She was also a member of Faith Impact Ministry.

Sister Doretta came into the beauty shop to have Sister Becky do her hair. Sister Becky was also Sister Doretta's sister-in-law. When Sister Doretta came in, she wasn't alone. She came over to us and introduced us to Sister Mindy.

Sister Becky and I said, "Hi."

They both sat down while Sister Doretta waited to get her hair done. Sister Becky and I noticed that they were acting as though they had known each other for a long time.

I could always sense the same spirit I was struggling with on another woman or girl. I did not know why Doretta was not aware that this spirit was in Sister Mindy. In my mind, I decided to prove to Sister Doretta that Sister Mindy was either active in the lesbian lifestyle or that she was not active.

Sister Mindy worked at the radio station at the time. She called me from the radio station one day. I felt this was my chance to expose that spirit I felt was in her.

I played along with Sister Mindy to catch her in the act so I could expose her to my friend, Sister Doretta. Things backfired on me. Sister Mindy went to Sister Doretta and told her I had hit on her. She declared that she was so hurt. She had just come to this church and thought this was where the Lord wanted her family to be.

For the first time in Sister Doretta's and my friendship, she got mad at me. What was happening in our relationship was very strange to me. She said I had lied and that I had not changed.

Sister Doretta, my closest friend, called Pastor Boyd and told him what Sister Mindy had said about me trying to come on to her. Pastor Boyd called a meeting with me before Bible Study began.

Pastor Boyd called me into his office and said he had received some disturbing news.

He said, "You told me that you were going to live a holy life now. Now, I hear that you said some inappropriate things to Sister Mindy."

He asked Sister Boyd to go and get Sister Mindy.

Sister Mindy came in like, "It was poor me. I have done no wrong."

I did not know what to expect from this meeting. Sister Mindy came in and sat in the chair beside me. Pastor Boyd was seated in his chair behind the desk; Sister Boyd stood by his side.

Pastor Boyd said, "Sister Mindy and her family are looking for a church home. They were contemplating joining our ministry. But she was disturbed by you approaching her in an improper way."

He then asked if I had said to Sister Mindy that I wanted to go with her. I told him that, yes, I did say that to her.

Everything was going through my mind. Sister Mindy had set me up. Even though she told them what she wanted them to know, I always took responsibility for my own actions. I was never one to tell someone else. Pastor Boyd never knew the whole story because I did not tell on Sister Mindy.

He told Sister Mindy that he was finished with her, and she could return to the Bible Study. Sister Mindy left the room and closed the door behind her. Pastor Boyd looked at me with such disappointment.

He said, "I thought you told me that you were going to do what is right. This must stop."

I just sat there with Sister Boyd in the room. I never said a word.

Pastor Boyd told me that all I could do from this point was at the altar until the Lord released me. I could not do anything in the ministry.

I held back the tears: ministry was my life. To not be able to do what I was called to do was like death to me.

Days, weeks, and months went by. I was on my knees at the altar crying out and praying to God to help me. But I also wanted that sister to be exposed. Doretta's and my relationship were never the same again.

I was very hurt by her. Concerning Sister Doretta's and my relationship, I felt within myself, "You have known me longer than this sister. How could you believe her over me?"

It was time for my deliverance, service. At first, they called Sister Laura in with us. Pastor Boyd began talking about deliverance; the demons that had begun to oppress me for so long began to manifest.

He looked at Sister Laura and said, "Now you see what you are dealing with."

Pastor Boyd had no idea that one time when they were on a revival trip, Sister Laura and I had gotten together in their home.

He told Sister Laura, "I do not want you calling Carla on the phone."

Laura left the building. It was just Pastor, Sister Boyd, and me left in the room. They began praying. Those spirits inside of me began to get uneasy. I began to breathe heavily. It was not me, although it was coming from me. Pastor sat behind his desk. He was so calm; he spoke firmly with authority.

He said, "You know that you have got to let her go."

A voice spoke out and said, "No."

The demons were getting angry with Pastor Boyd.

The demonic voices answered and told him, "I am not leaving. I have been here since she was a child."

Sister Boyd was silently praying within herself. The demons began to expose some things about her past.

She said, "Yes, devil. Jesus has forgiven me, and it is covered under the Blood."

Most people believe that when someone is doing a deliverance service with a person that you are not aware of what is going on. That is false. I knew everything that was going on even though the things coming out of my mouth were not coming from me. The demons were using my mouth to say what they wanted to say.

Foam began to come from my mouth. There was a foul odor. Hours went by. Neither Pastor nor Sister Boyd ever raised their voices. They simply spoke with authority.

When the deliverance was finished, they gave me some instructions. I still could not work in the ministry until God released me, though.

Time went by. I asked Pastor Boyd if I could return to working in the ministry.

He said, "When the Lord says so; then and only then. You just stay in prayer."

Finally, God released me to go back to work in the ministry. I was so glad. All the time that I couldn't do any work, I felt that Pastor Boyd and God were mad with me.

The truth never came out about Sister Mindy. I never mentioned what truly happened between us. I knew better than to bring the incident up. I should have never tried to set the sister up. God was not pleased with the way I tried to do things my way.

Through Sister Laura, I met a minister: Nathan Curry. We became good friends. I became fond of Minister Nathan and felt that he was beginning to like me as well. I invited him to my house for dinner. He accepted my invitation.

I planned the dinner for Saturday evening. Although I was very nervous, I was also very excited. I didn't have many relationships in my life. I wanted this to be the perfect dinner for him. I cooked. Minister Nathan came that evening at about 5 PM. My table was set for a king.

After we talked a while, I asked Minister Nathan if he was ready to eat.

He said, "Yes."

We went to the table; he sat down. I went into the kitchen to fix his plate. I put the plate in front of him and went back into the kitchen to fix my plate.

As we ate and talked, he complimented me on the food.

I said, "Thank you."

We had a very good time that evening. We decided to have another fellowship for Christmas. When Minister Nathan left, I was boiling over with joy and excitement.

I had at least two months to get my Christmas decorations and prepare my menu for our dinner. Minister Nathan called me often.

We would talk about the Lord for a long time. Minister Nathan was courteous, a kindhearted man of God.

December seemed to have come very quickly. I was ready. I had a beautiful Christmas tree that was decorated with different colored lights. My table was set up with a red tablecloth, green napkins, and a red candle with green leaves around the candle. I had a pinecone centerpiece on my end table. Everything was so beautiful in my house. Plus, I had a Christmas gift for Minister Nathan.

Our dinner was that week before Christmas. I had purchased a beautiful red dress and black shoes to wear for our dinner. Sister Becky did my hair. I had my nails and toes done also on that Thursday morning.

Saturday morning, I went to Kroger's to get the things for the meal I was going to cook that day. My menu was baked honey ham, cornbread dressing, green beans, cranberry sauce, potato salad, cake, and ice cream. I purchased everything I needed to prepare my meal for that night.

I began preparing my meal. I was excited but a little afraid because I wanted everything to be perfect. The time had come. Unfortunately, Minister Nathan never showed up for our Christmas dinner date. Nor did he answer his phone. Tears rolled down my face. I had never felt such hurt as I did that day. I never heard from Minister Nathan after that day.

My Auntie Roberson moved to Texas. My cousin, her daughter, began attending now-Pastor Nathan's church. Through her, I found out what had happened that Christmas day when Minister Nathan failed to show up for our dinner date.

Sister Mason was one of our prayer warriors at Faith Impact Full Gospel Church. She was very jealous of my relationship with Pastor Marvin T. & Kathleen Boyd.

Rumors must have come to Sister Mason that I liked women. We were all attending Faith Impact Full Gospel Church at the time. Again, Sister Mason was extremely jealous of my relationship with the pastors.

At that time, I had lived with the Boyd's for five years, taking care of their home and their sons. By the time Minister Nathan and I were talking, I was living in my own apartment. I didn't know that my hair stylist, Sister Dolly, knew Minister Nathan. She had done my hair on several occasions. She and I were not friends but were acquainted. Our relationship was based on her doing my hair and being Sisters-in-the-Lord. I do not know how Auntie Roberson obtained her information that Minister Nathan and I were talking.

I was not aware that Sister Mason and Sister Dolly were friends. Sister Dolly told my cousin that she had heard that I liked girls, and that Minister Nathan had broken up with me after he found out about my past through Sister Dolly. Minister Nathan decided to never see or talk to me again. He ended up marrying Sister Dolly.

One day I was visiting Auntie Roberson. She shared with me what Sister Dolly had told her daughter: that she found out I had been living a lesbian lifestyle.

About five years passed. One day, our church had to visit another church because our pastor had to preach that evening. To my surprise, who else but now-Pastor Nathan and Sister Dolly came through the door as the service was going on? All those feelings I had felt that day all came back, rushing over me. I had turned around, and we looked straight into each other's faces. I forced myself to hold back the tears and the emotion I felt inside.

Pastor Nathan and his wife came close to the front of the sanctuary. They sat three seats behind me. I looked back a little but kept my focus on the service as best I could. When they started taking up the offering, he and his wife went around the table. We all looked at each other, face to face, politely speaking to each other. Although I really didn't want to speak, I felt it was the right thing to do.

In my heart, I felt like, "You knew I was interested in you. You should have respected me enough to tell me why you stood me up and why you never answered your phone when I tried to call you that day for our dinner date the night before Christmas."

All those thoughts rushed through my mind. After the church service was over, Sister Dolly went around the sanctuary to fellowship with some of the other believers.

Pastor Nathan pushed away from the other saints. He got to me and began trying to talk to me. I asked him how married life was. He told me that it was alright. I could tell from how he responded that all wasn't going so well.

I told him, "You chose her over me and never looked back. You really hurt me. I never thought you were the kind of Man of God who would have done me that way."

He could not say a word to me on the subject. His wife Dolly came over when she saw him talking to me. We embraced as sisters. I walked away from both and didn't see them again for many years.

My greatest fear had come true. I had never wanted to get involved with any man because I felt that, once they knew about my past, they would run away from me as fast as possible. With Nathan, that came true.

Chapter 12

The Abused Becomes the Abuser

After I stopped working for Mrs. Belinda Tate, I started taking babysitting jobs with several Caucasian families. I worked for the Bowden family and kept their 5-month-old son, Benjamin.

I also worked for the Robertson family who had adopted a baby boy. Jeremiah was 5 months old when I began working for his family and taking care of him. The Robertson's lived in a beautiful house in Baytown, Texas, in a very nice subdivision.

Mr. and Mrs. Robertson left for work at 7 AM every morning. I had to be there by 6 AM. Jeremiah was a very spoiled baby. They let him have his way. They were unable to control Jeremiah's behavior. I believe because Jeremiah was adopted, they were trying to do everything right as parents.

As soon as the Robertson's came home from work every day, the first thing they did was go to the bar for a drink. Then, they would ask me to take Jeremiah for several hours. Jeremiah knew he could not and would not get away with treating me like he did his parents.

I became firm with Jeremiah. I let him know straight-up that temper tantrums were not acceptable. He would run his head into the door and fall completely out onto the floor, screaming.

I brought Jeremiah to church with me. Everyone there took turns holding him, and he became the church baby. One Sunday while we were in service and Pastor was on the podium and everything was quiet, suddenly out of nowhere, Jeremiah opened his mouth and said, "Amen." Everyone laughed. The service took off and the people began to rejoice in the Lord.

I realized one day, though, that something was wrong with me. I had fixed Jeremiah some fish sticks, fries, and given him some juice for lunch. He went into his mode of not wanting to eat his food. I became impatient with him and kept telling him, "Eat your food. It is good."

I tried to feed him; he spit it out. I became very angry with Jeremiah and started force feeding the food down his throat until he began choking. He tried to spit the food out; I continued forcing the food into his mouth. I froze. I could not believe what I was doing. I became scared. I got out the phone book and looked up *Texas Children Protective Service*. I called and pretended I was reporting a person that was abusing a child.

The TCPS told me I needed to turn this person in to the authorities.

I quickly hung up the phone, took Jeremiah into my arms, and began telling him how sorry I was for treating him the way I was. Because of my behavior, I rocked him to sleep instead of putting him into his bed to go to sleep on his own. I felt so bad about what I had done, and what I could have done.

The Robertson's had no idea why Jeremiah obeyed me and not them. Although he feared me, he did not know how to relate to his parents. I loved Jeremiah. He was with me about 85% of the time. His parents were afraid to discipline him. Because they allowed him to do whatever he wanted, he gave them a lot of trouble.

For one summer, I traveled with the Robertson's on their vacation to Camden, Alabama. The main reason for me accompanying them was because they did not know how to handle their son. I received double the salary for that trip.

During our trip, Jeremiah did not sleep in the same room as his parents: he slept in the room with me. Even though the Robertson's had adopted him, they spent less time with Jeremiah. They continued to have a drink after work before they could handle their son.

They called me during the holidays and asked if I would pick Jeremiah up and give them a break. That's when I received the news that Mark's job was transferring him to Camden, Alabama. They wanted me to move down there with them. I told them I could not leave my church home. However, I did agree to go with them for a month. I helped them get set up, put things in order, and watched Jeremiah.

I traveled back and forth to Alabama to visit several times whenever they needed me to take care of Jeremiah and clean their house. They traveled to Baytown for their jobs, and we would meet up with Jeremiah. He still remembered me even as he grew older.

During this time, I became involved with Faith Impact Full Gospel Ministry under the leadership of Pastors Marvin T. and Kathleen Boyd.

My Cousin Tammy was having problems in her life. She could not take care of her three-year-old daughter, Joy, and asked if I would keep Joy until she could get on her feet. I told her yes.

At that time, I was babysitting John and Jill Hamilton's three children: Samantha, Billy, and Betty, in Baytown. Joy lived with me in my one-bedroom apartment at Greenwood Apartments on Tompkins Road. I had to be at work at 8 AM every day. Every morning, I got up at 6 AM to get Joy up and ready. While she was at the table eating breakfast, I took my shower and got dressed.

Usually when I was ready to go, Joy was not finished with her breakfast because she ate very slowly. This made me mad. I told Joy we were going to get up two hours earlier because I could not allow her to make me late for work.

One day while I was picking Joy up from daycare, the teacher, Mrs. Brown, called me over to discuss Joy. Joy was not playing with the other children during play time. Mrs. Brown asked why. I told her I did not know why, but I would talk to Joy about it when we got home.

Until that moment, I had never really noticed how clean Joy was when I picked her up from school. Even her hair was still in place. I did not realize I had put so much fear into Joy about keeping her clothes clean by telling her, "They better not be dirty, and you had better not lose any barrettes out of your hair."

The Holy Spirit brought this incident to my mind. Joy was afraid I was going to beat her if she got dirt on her clothes or lost her hair barrettes. When I was made aware of what I was doing, I asked Joy to forgive me. I assured her that it was alright to play with the other children at daycare.

I still did not totally understand what was going on with me, though. Materially, Joy did not want for anything. I made sure she had everything she needed. Unfortunately, I did not know how to genuinely love her. I could only show love to her by getting things for her.

Some of the brothers and sisters at Faith Impact Ministry told me I was too hard on Joy; she was only 3 years old. The other children would be running and playing outside, sometimes even inside of the church. Joy had to sit down wherever I placed her and not move until I was ready to go. Because she was so accustomed to my threats, she knew not to move from her seat until I came to remove her.

One week when school was out for the summer, I asked the Hamilton's if I could bring Joy to work with me. They told me, "Carla, you know that will be alright."

Because I usually got Joy up at 5 AM during the school year to get ready to leave our home, I was now able to tell her, "Joy, you have all the time you need now to eat."

When we arrived at the Hamilton's home on one particular day, Samantha, 13, Betty, 6, and Billy, 4, were all still in bed. I let Joy watch cartoons until the children woke up. Mr. and Mrs. Hamilton left for work.

While the children were still sleeping and Joy was watching cartoons, I went into Mr. and Mrs. Hamilton's room, took the sheets off the bed, the towels off the floor in the bedroom, and started the washing machine. When I passed through the living room, Joy had fallen asleep on the sofa while looking at cartoons. I covered her with a small blanket.

I went into the kitchen, put the dishes in the dishwasher, and started cleaning the Master Bedroom and bathroom. Samantha, Betty, and Billy were still asleep.

The children all woke up at about 10:30 AM. They went into the living room when I told them that Joy was there. They were so excited to see Joy. Joy was also happy to see them again. I fixed pancakes, bacon, and eggs for them for breakfast, and gave them orange juice to drink.

While the children ate, I went to their rooms and stripped their beds. After they finished eating, Samantha went into her room to get dressed. I went in with Betty and Billy to their rooms to get their clothes out. I made sure they brushed their teeth and combed their hair.

As I cleaned the house, the smaller children played in the backyard; Samantha watched television in the living room. About 11:30, I asked what they all wanted for lunch. They all said pizza. I took a large pizza out of the freezer. I told them if they ate all their pizza, I would give them the dessert of their choice.

They ate all their pizza. Samantha wanted a chocolate cupcake; Betty wanted candy; Billy and Joy wanted a vanilla ice cream cone. After they finished, it was time for their nap. I had finished cleaning the house, and only needed to finish washing and folding the laundry.

After about two hours, Samantha called me, "Carla."

I answered back, "Samantha."

She said, "I need to tell you something."

These children knew me to a certain point when it came to dealing with them.

She said to me, "Do not spank Joy, please."

I asked, "Samantha, what is going on. Why are you asking me to not spank Joy? What has Joy done?"

Samantha got Joy from the bedroom. Joy was crying. I did not know why.

I asked, "What is wrong with you, Joy?"

Samantha said, "Joy wet the bed."

I guess you could say that the horn poked out of my head.

I said, "What?"

All I could see and hear was that Joy had wet Samantha's bed. I looked at Joy in anger. You could see the fear on both the girls' faces.

I told Joy, "You know better than that. Why did you not go to the bathroom?"

Joy cried even harder.

"Why did you not go to the bathroom and use it?" By then, my tone had elevated.

Joy trembled, but I kept going at her.

I told her, "I am going to beat you!"

When I reached to grab her arm, Samantha said, "No, Carla!"

But I was not listening to a child!

At that moment, the Lord allowed me to hear myself for the first time. But it was not my voice; it was the voice of my Mama, Bessie. I realized right then that I had become my mother, the abuser. I knew I could not beat Joy. The Lord told me to not touch her. I fell to the floor, screaming, tears rolling down my face.

"I am sorry, Joy. I did not know."

I softly gathered Joy into my arms. I asked her to forgive me. This child, I believe, understood. She hugged me back as well as Samantha who was on the floor crying with us. The Lord was using Samantha.

She said, "Carla, the Lord has forgiven you. You did not know."

She hugged me tightly. The Hamilton's are a Christian family. Their children knew about Jesus, and forgiveness, especially Samantha.

Betsy and Billy came into the room. We all cried. From that day on, I never raised a hand to touch Joy again.

In 1994, I went to live with Pastor Marvin T. and Kathleen Boyd and their four sons: Daniel, 13; Marvin, 10; Micah, 8; and Ben, 3.

Pastor Marvin T. Boyd, Sr.: Words can't describe the anointing on this man's life. When he entered the building, you knew he had been with God.

Pastor Boyd was a man of integrity. He was humble and gave God's people so much love. He was a man of God who was given to much prayer. He was also a scholar of the Word of God. The same way Pastor Boyd was in public, was the same way he was at home.

I was privileged to be in the house of one of the greatest Apostles, Prophets, Evangelists, Pastors, Teachers, and prayer warriors in the

Holy Ghost on the face of the earth. At the house of God, he was Pastor. At home, he was Dad. It was a blessing to me to have the opportunity to serve him in all his capacities.

I watched how Pastor Boyd interacted with his sons. He loved his sons with all his heart. I watched the boys and how they enjoyed playing and laughing with their Dad. I loved how they went out together and spent quality time with each other as a family.

The boys were especially excited when their parents returned home from revival meetings. It never failed! Whenever Pastor and Lady Boyd returned from ministering for two weeks at a revival, they would give time to their boys before they even tried to rest.

And let me tell you about Sister Boyd: she is just such a sweet person. When she hugs you, you feel the love, genuine love. I did not understand her type of love.

Many times, she would tell the boys to go and clean their rooms. They would go up to their rooms and push everything under their beds and into the closet.

I knew that was what they did because when I went up there to put their clothes away after doing laundry, I checked to see if they had done what they were supposed to do. Instead, they had pushed everything under the beds and into their closets.

The boys would let the trash pile up in the kitchen. They would half clean the bathroom and leave dirty dishes on the table. They did not clean up their messes! I would get so mad when I saw Sister Boyd hugging those disobedient boys. I felt like her boys did not deserve to be hugged. They never completely did what they were told to do in the right way. The only form of discipline I was accustomed to was beating, hollering, and verbal abuse.

I recall Mama telling Carl and me, "You are hardheaded, stubborn, and you are the worst two children I have."

I was not accustomed to parents hugging and showing affection to their children. This was something I had never experienced.

I even asked Sister Boyd, "Why don't you beat them?"

I wanted her to stop all that hugging and kissing. I did not realize that the love she was showing me was the same love she gave to her sons.

I had a real problem with children resulting in me being so hard on them. I did not show affection because there had always been a lack of affection in my home.

Pastor Marvin and Sister Kathleen not only told me they loved me, though, they showed it. Despite my shortcomings, they looked beyond my faults and saw my needs. It was the same as the love and chastisement I had experienced through the Word of God. I was so blessed to have spiritual parents in my life like Pastor Marvin T. and Sister Kathleen Boyd.

I hid nothing from my leaders. I was very honest with them concerning the things I was struggling with in my life. They gave me Biblical counseling and took me through deliverance. I truly thank God for Sister Kathleen Boyd.

At home, she was Mama. But Sister Boyd was more than my Pastor's wife. At times, I looked to her as a friend and big sister all wrapped up in one package. There was nothing I couldn't share with this Woman of God. Even after all these years, Sister Boyd is still a woman given to much prayer and the Word of God. During the time I was with them, she showed me what unconditional love was by how she loved her sons.

I was also the type of person who demanded respect. There was something in me that would not allow a child to disrespect me in any way. Because of that, I was very hard on children. My parents were hard on me. I didn't know how to love or be affectionate.

Today, I am still a perfectionist to a certain degree. God's not through with me yet, though. I am allowing Him to complete me in every area of my life. I have been hard on myself all of my life. That was what I was accustomed to. That was how my parents dealt with me as I grew up in their home.

In 1995, I formed a drill team in Faith Impact Ministry. You would have thought I had previously served in the Army. I was like an Army Drill Sergeant to those children. Some of the children had tender hearts; I did not know that. They were so afraid of me; they would start crying when I was instructing or speaking to them.

Some of the parents felt that their children needed to be toughened up, so they allowed me to be hard on their children. We practiced on Saturdays at 12 PM.

Before I moved in with the Boyd's, I had this old, ancient brown Ford. I paid $300.00 for that car. I bought it from someone in my neighborhood, but did not know that the window was sealed with tar to keep the rain from coming in. The car had a hole on the right side of the driver's seat in the back.

On Saturday, I would go to Baytown and start picking up my children for Drill Team practice. I would fill the car up with as many children as I could. My trunk was so big; I had children sitting in the trunk. During that time, Baytown was not as commercial as it is now. I was never pulled over by the cops. I believe God hid me because my heart was in the right place.

I provided hot dogs, chips, and sodas for the kids. Sometimes, I would have enough money to buy burger meals for them. But they worked hard for those meals! I would take them over the drills about 10 to 15 times from 12 PM until 3 PM before they were allowed to eat their meals.

I did not allow too many mess ups after I had given them sufficient time to learn the drills and to memorize 200 scriptures: the Ten Commandments and books of the Bible from Genesis to Revelation. I memorized all I asked them to learn in two weeks; I gave them two months to memorize everything.

I searched for different ministries with whom we could go and fellowship. We performed with other drill teams that were on the programs. The Drill Team was the highlight of the ministry.

When we had a program and the Drill Team had on their uniforms, they performed from recorded music. They were sharp. The audience and parents stood in excitement as the Drill Team performed. Many times, we had other church drill teams there to perform as well.

I was very hard on the children because of what I had experienced. I did not know I had become just like my parents, Jimmy and Bessie.

When Pastor and Sister Boyd had to go out on the field to evangelize, their boys were not happy. They knew they were going to be in the Army with Carla. We would get the house sparkling clean, and it would stay that way until I was no longer in authority.

My 4-year-old niece, Jennifer, came to live with me. She was my baby brother Michael's daughter. Jennifer was stubborn, and already molded and set in her ways like I was when I was a little girl. But I was going to prove to her that I was the **Queen of Stubborn**. I would tell her to go left; she went right. I would tell her to go right; she went left. It was just like when I was a child with my mother.

Jennifer needed a lot of training. Coming from a dysfunctional family, though, she mostly needed love. Michael was drinking and on drugs and was still a very selfish person. He did not look out for Jennifer and was never really a father to her. Her mother, Jose, was also on drugs, resulting in Jennifer learning the streets at an early age.

When I came into Jennifer's life, Jose had left her at the front door of Michael's apartment without even checking if Michael was there. Of course, he was not at home.

Although I was aware of God placing me with people who showed me so much love and did not judge me for the struggles I was having in my life, I could not share the same with others. I could not see that effect in my life and how I should share it with Jennifer and others.

Jennifer had street sense, something I was not accustomed to. When she did things I did not understand, I did not understand why I became angry with her. The only way I knew how to deal with her issues was to beat her. Beating Jennifer made her much worse. I became the same way.

I told Jennifer that when she answered me, she was to say, 'Yes, Ma'am,' and 'No, Ma'am." Because she was not accustomed to saying these things, she resorted back to what she was accustomed to saying.

I gave Jennifer a month to learn to say, 'Yes, Ma'am,' and, 'No, Ma'am.'

After that month, though, she slipped and said, 'No. Unn huh, yea,'

I hit her right in the place she said it: her mouth. I did not know that was a form of abuse at the time. Remember: that was the same treatment my parents had given to me.

I bought Jennifer's clothes from the boutique for children. She had lace socks that matched everything she wore. The parents at church wanted to know where I shopped for her clothes. Jennifer also had pretty barrettes that matched everything from her head to her toes, and she always carried a cute little purse.

I enrolled Jennifer in different activities during the summer while I was at work. I made sure she had every toy and doll you could think of. This was the only way I could express love to her.

One time when we were shopping at the mall, I looked around and Jennifer walked away from me. I had to break her out of that habit because that was dangerous. Someone could have taken her. At the time, I did not know that sometimes you could just talk to children. No one ever talked to me; they just beat me.

Jose came back into Jennifer's life. She had gotten off drugs and wanted her daughter back home with her. Because of my own issues of not having a mother, Jennifer had become my security by then.

She was doing great with me, but I let her go back to her Mama's house. Unfortunately, some things had not changed in Jose's life. Jennifer was able to express some of the street life she had already tasted.

Jennifer began getting into trouble all the time in school; she would call me to help her. I wanted her to move in with me, but I was living with my lover's family. They did not want Jennifer to live in their home. I would take her over the weekend and keep her in the room I was living in at the time with my family.

After three years, Jennifer came back to live with me. Jose was back on drugs. Sadly, though, Aunt Carla was having a hard time with this go-round with Jennifer.

I was living in Brook Cove Apartments in Houston, Texas. Jennifer was 14 years old when she moved back in with me. I was a member of Lily of the Valley Apostolic Church in Houston, under the leadership of Pastor Brenda G. Jones.

Chapter 13

No Good Thing in My Flesh

I felt that this was the lowest I had fallen in my walk with God.

No longer living with the Boyd family, I had my own apartment on Westheimer and Fondren. I was also still operating "**Leave it to Beaver Cleaning Service;**" things were going great.

Let me back up a little so you won't get lost in what I am about to share.

Before I moved to Houston, I lived in Baytown, right down the street from the church. Brother Wilbert and Brother Kyle Johnson and his wife Sarah were members of Faith Impact Ministry. We all became best friends. When we had revivals that lasted for a week, instead of them going back to their homes in Houston, they stayed over at my place through the weekend. Brothers Wilbert and Kyle slept in the front room on the couch and the floor. Sister Sarah and I slept in my bedroom.

At the time, I did not know that Brother Kyle, Sister Sarah's husband, liked me. I was unaware of his feelings towards me.

The Saints at church were trying to hook Brother Wilbert and me together. Brother Wilbert was not someone I was interested in because he was not strong in his faith in the Lord. Many times, he wanted me to cater to his ways. That made me a little angry. I knew that our relationship was not going to end in a good way because he was very demanding.

While the Johnsons and Brother Wilbert were guests in my home, I did all the cooking. Brother Johnson would say little things I thought were inappropriate. Many times, I had to correct him because I felt that what he was saying to me was hurtful to Sister Sarah.

One time while Sister Sarah was sitting right there in the room, he said if he had met me first, he would have married me. I rebuked him right in front of his wife. I knew what he said did not make her feel good. Sister Johnson was such a kind, sweet person; she would hurt no one.

Mama even knew Brother Johnson liked me because he had made it known to her. Brother Johnson and I would have little disputes. Sister Boyd, my Pastor's wife also knew there was something there. She often made me aware.

Time went by.

One night, I received a phone call from one of the ministers and his wife about Brother Johnson. They told me that they were calling me to warn me to be watchful. They told me that Brother Johnson really liked me, and I needed to be careful.

At that time, I was dealing with some feelings I had never dealt with before. I guess you can say that my body was in heat.

I did not know how to handle myself. I would come home from work, fill the tub with warm water, put my head under the water, and scream, "Help me, Lord. I do not know what is wrong with me and why I am feeling this way."

I cannot tell you when Brother Johnson and I started talking privately for long hours as we were doing our business.

One Saturday, Dad, Pastor Boyd, came home. He said, "Carla, Brother Johnson likes you, but you cannot touch that. He is married."

Brother Johnson called me every day; sometimes three or four times a day. Our conversations became intimate. My body had never felt so aroused.

One day, we decided to meet up, get in one car, and just ride somewhere. We met that night. I got into his vehicle. We talked and rode around for half the night. I did not realize that I had so much confidence in my flesh - I was so self-righteous and very selfish - until God exposed me. I was not thinking about Sister Johnson even though I was listening to her talk about her husband.

I told her they both needed to get some marriage counseling from Pastor and Sister Boyd. Her husband was telling me everything I desired to hear from a Man of God; a man who really loved me. He would tell me things no other man had ever said to me.

I thought, "This man is really in love with me."

Yes, I knew he was married. But he told me that I made him feel like a real man and he wanted to be with me. I listened to his pain and his wife's pain all at the same time. The entire time Brother Johnson was talking to me, I was betraying his wife. And yet, I was also trying to counsel both to get some help for their marriage.

What kind of friend was I, talking to her and to her husband at the same time? I had never felt so low. And yet, a part of me wanted this to be real.

There was a drive in me that did not want to stop talking to Brother Johnson. I had never heard of phone sex until I started listening to him. He seduced me over the telephone. I had to tell somebody, so I told Irma, Paula, and Mike. These were what you could call *true* friends. They never breathed a word to anyone about what was going on between Brother Johnson and me.

Brother Kyle and Sister Sarah were connected to a ministry that allowed Pastors to go to a place of solitude to fast and pray. They talked to the minister and let them know that I was a minister. So, they let me go to the cabin to fast and pray. I did not want to fall in this way.

I stayed at the cabin for a week. I was crying out to God to deliver me from this.

"I do not want to do this. I do not want to hurt Sister Johnson!"

It seemed like all of that was in vain, though. Brother Johnson and I began talking on the phone while I was there. On Sunday, he came to my room. My flesh was on fire.

I told him, "You must stop coming to my classroom, please." He would come to my Sunday School classroom to talk to me.

I was doing everything I could to avoid our getting close. I finally decided to let Brother Johnson come to my house. I had purchased razor blades, deodorant, a comb and brush, toothpaste, cologne, tee shirts, underwear, and gym pants in case he needed to take a shower at my house. After he got off work one night, I let him come over and take a shower. We spent some time together.

Always honest with my leaders, I had to let them know that things were getting out of control.

Sister Kathleen Boyd and I went to a restaurant. I told her what was going on between Brother Johnson and me. She asked if Brother Johnson had been to my house. I told her he had and that I had fallen in love with him.

Pastor Marvin and Sister Kathleen Boyd set up a meeting with Brother Johnson and me. Pastor was not happy about this situation.

He rebuked Brother Johnson. "What are you doing? You are a married man."

Brother Johnson replied, "I fell in love with Carla."

Pastor Boyd told us, "You both are leaders in the ministry. This must stop or I will have to involve Sister Johnson."

The more Pastor Boyd talked, the angrier I became. Brother Johnson and I had formed soul-ties. Part of me did not want this to stop even though I knew what we were doing was wrong.

I asked Pastor Boyd, "Could I go to Sandpiper Church for a while? Let the Saints pray with me until I get victory in this area."

So many people had already left Faith Impact Ministry. I believe Pastor thought that if I left for a season, I would not come back. I made this request the same week we were having a tent revival. Pastor needed me to help during the revival. I wanted so much to be at the altar crying out to God to help me out of this mess I had put myself into. God moved in the revival; souls were saved!

That week, I was just going through the motions. I did not feel good about what I was doing. I felt that God was angry with me. After the revival, I decided to call Brother Johnson.

I told him, "Let's do this."

I prepared myself. I had watched so many love movies where the couples were very intimate with each other. I placed rose petals all over the floor all the way to the bedroom and in the bed at my home.

Love music played in the background. I had on sexy red lingerie. I sprayed on my favorite perfume, White Diamond.

I was 38 years old and knew nothing about a man making love to me or me making love to a man. All I knew was that it was the worst time of my life. I simply acted like I was having a good time while pleasing Brother Johnson.

Afterward, we took a shower. He got dressed and left. I cried all night long; what I had just done was wrong. Now I wanted to think about Sister Johnson. This thing was eating me alive.

At this time, I thought Sister Laura was my best friend. I thought I could trust her. I shared with her that Brother Johnson and I had failed. We had gone too far.

As soon as we hung up the phone, she obviously could not wait to call Pastor Boyd and share what I had just shared with her.

I received a phone call from Sister Boyd. "I guess now you are going to live right?"

Brother Johnson called. I was so upset, I told him, "If I am pregnant,

I will leave and won't let you know."

He decided to share with his wife that he and I had slept together. On that same day, I received another call. It was Sister Johnson.

She said, "How could you?"

I heard the hurt in her voice. For a moment, I was silent.

Then I said, "I am so sorry. Please forgive me."

Sister Johnson hung up the phone. I could not stop crying. I could not sleep. I would work and cry all day.

All I could say was, "How could I have done this thing?"

Both my leaders were extremely disappointed. Neither Pastor Marvin T. nor Sister Kathleen Boyd would speak to me. It would not have hurt so badly if I had not looked at Pastor Boyd as a father figure in my life. If I ever needed a father, now would have been a good time for him to step up to the plate.

Although I understood that they both had to be there for Sister Johnson, I had never felt so all alone in my life. I thought that God felt the same way about me as the Pastor did. I could not even pray. Nothing would come out of my mouth.

I kept crying because I did not know how to pray. The Spirit of God gave me songs in the form of prayers. That is how I prayed.

As time went by, I started writing letters to Pastor Boyd. Sister Boyd would deliver them to him from me. Pastor never responded to those letters. I would get up and do my business through fasting and praying. I stayed before the Lord like never before.

I had lost a true friend in Sister Johnson. I knew I could never look her in the face again; she would never look at me the same again.

And I still felt guilty. Once again, I shared with another friend I thought I could trust. She shared what I told her with one of the other ministers in the church. He is called Brother Johnson. I received a call from him: he was angry. I told him I was not going around telling people. I found out who was spreading the story. The ceiling hit the fan when the whole church found out what Brother Johnson and I had done.

The last words Pastor Boyd spoke to me were when he called me to his office. He asked me to come back to the church. I told him that would be impossible knowing that the Johnson's were members.

Through this incident, I had lost the respect of the Body of Christ. Some rejoiced because they had always felt that Pastor Boyd had put me on a pedestal.

Many of them were now saying, "Look at her now!"

Some *true* friends even stopped fellowshipping with me. I couldn't blame them, though. I had stepped off the path.

Then, I found out that Pastor and Sister Boyd were moving back to Denver. Some of the Saints called to let me know. They were hurt that Pastor Boyd and Sister Boyd were leaving Faith Impact Ministry.

After they left, I did not go to church for about a year. I finally visited John Henry Ministry and became a member. I still had my business, *Leave It to Beaver Cleaning Service*. I was doing a lot of fasting and praying. I felt that the Lord wanted me to do a 5-day and night revival.

I shared this with Pastor Thomas. He said he would support me all the way. I rented the civic building in Baytown. I found out that Pastor Brenda Jones, a pastor I had met through Evangelist Candy, had decided to let her members support me but only Evangelist Candy and Sister Beverly of Rock Holiness Church of God In Christ were there to support me.

Chapter 14
Unnatural Affection

Romans 1:26-27 AMPC *For this reason God gave them over and abandoned them to vile affections and degrading passions. For their women exchanged their natural function for an unnatural and abnormal one, 27 And the men also turned from natural relations with women and were set ablaze (burning out, consumed) with lust for one another – men committing shameful acts with men and suffering in their own bodies and personalities the inevitable consequences and penalty of their wrong-doing and going astray, which was [their] fitting retribution.*

In 2001, I attended True Life Church in Houston, Texas. I was giving myself to prayer, the Word of God, and fasting. I felt in my spirit that the Holy Spirit was leading me to do a revival. I shared this with my pastor, and he gave me the okay to have it in Baytown, Texas, at the Civic Center.

Two of my ministering friends attended my revival those three nights. After the revival, we stopped by my mother's house; she served us what she had cooked. I met a woman in Baytown, Mrs. Beverly, and we began to eat out at different places in Houston.

I began to realize the lesbian spirit that I dealt with was just lying dormant.

I would share many things with my friend Mrs. Beverely about the things I had done with other women in my past. She listened to me and never judged me; we became close friends. I began to be attracted to Mrs. Beverely; I even told her that, if women would listen too closely, I had a seducing spirit that could charm the pants of anyone who is weak or dealing with a spirit of lust.

I was making good money at the time, and even though I didn't voice my feelings at the time to Mrs. Beverely, I would shower her with many gifts.

Mrs. Beveryly and I didn't live in the same part of the city, but we did many things together. Whatever I brought myself in the store, I did the same for Mrs. Beverely.

I would send Mrs. Beverely teddy bears, candy, and flowers delivered to her job. I was always expressing the love I had inside for Mrs. Beverely. In my other relationship with women, I would cry because I felt so convicted.

Until one of my partners couldn't take it anymore and broke our relationship off. I was so in love with Mrs. Beverly but too afraid to tell her verbally. I would keep showering her with gifts, even money.

Most women that I was involved with were a few years older than I was. The love I felt for Mrs. Beverely was that I wanted to be with her all the time; I would lay out the carpet for this woman.

I began to buy her expensive jewelry, and she was so grateful; I always made what I did for Mrs. Beverely very sensual.

I wanted her to see how deeply in love I am, and I wanted to take things to another level. I was mostly walking on eggshells because I knew that Mrs. Beverely was straight, and I didn't want to lose the relationship I had with her.

Sometimes, when she touches me so tenderly, I would burn in my flesh, wanting more of her touch. I knew if she would let her guard down for one second, that seducing spirit would take over, and she would fall under his spell.

I believe the reason I began to open to my flesh is that when my pastor, Marvin T. & Kathleen Boyd, moved back to Denver, Colorado, it left an even bigger void in my life. Also, I was still self-beating myself for all the pain I caused before my leader moved.

Mrs. Beverely was a few years older than me; I always was starving for the love of a mother; the enemy used this to his advantage in my life. When I would share things with Mrs. Beverely, I would warn her not to listen to me because of that seducing spirit.

I believe that those spirits that were oppressing me became stronger, and the more I wanted to do what was right, I still wanted to be intimate with Mrs. Beverely. It didn't matter what time of day it was when Mrs. Beverely needed me; I would run to aide her in whatever she needed.

When you keep practicing sin, you fall deeper and deeper into things you never thought you would do. I knew that the purpose for me doing the thing I did was in the hope that the same love I gave to that person would be returned to me in the same way. Instead, life ended up with me being the person doing all the giving and never receiving. I convinced myself that my happiness came from making the other person happy.

Mrs. Beverely and I finally took the next level; all that I did paid off things I said no to; I was saying yes. I felt that it was my job to make her happy in every part of her life. Eventually, though, continually pouring into and giving out began not to feel so good to me anymore.

I found myself wanting the same thing that Mrs. Beverely needed. I knew that we both wanted the same thing in a relationship: to be in love. Finally, we decided to become roommates, and that worked out for a while. Everything seemed to be great in both of our lives.

After many years passed, Mrs. Beverely changed from this caring person to this mean person. She began to treat me with so much anger, and I didn't know why. One of my biggest mistakes was us becoming roommates. Many don't realize the hell I went through in this relationship.

After Mrs. Beverely's change, and not knowing what brought about the change. I still was not ready to let her go. I felt if I had stayed in my own apartment, I would not have lost everything I worked so hard to accomplish.

No matter how kind I was to her, she even became furious with whatever I did. I told her that her treatment of me was very hurtful. It became evident that she didn't care about me anymore. Many nights, I cried and prayed, asking God to get me out of this situation I had put myself in.

The loneliness was so overbearing and overpowering that I started taking my prescribed medicine more than I was supposed to so I could just sleep and never wake up. I knew about rejection, but not like I experienced through this relationship. I just wanted to forget about the distance that was between Mrs. Beverely and I.

No one knew the torment I dealt with day and night. Who could I share my pain with? Many nights, I cried myself to sleep because of the loneliness. Every night, I tossed and turned. I was still holding on to the belief that she would change.

I thought maybe because I didn't have the money I had when I first met Mrs. Beverely, that's what caused her to change. The little change I had, when I went in the store and bought some things, I would bring her one of the same items.

I thought she would start loving me again, but that didn't happen. Our relationship was over. I didn't know how to let her go. It was hard being in her presence. I never knew the right things to say that wouldn't trigger her anger.

I caught myself wondering, "Does anyone see what is going on? Why want someone that doesn't make the pain go away? Why am I being treated so coldly?

I knew that I had to separate from her. I knew I had to get away from this kind of abuse. All I had was my disability check. That wasn't enough to pay rent for an apartment. My credit was very poor. Only God knew the hell I was going through inside.

I went to my own sister and asked her if I could stay with her until I was able to get my own place.

She told me that she just had been bored and that right now she couldn't let me stay with her.

I asked Mama, and she turned me away as well.

I asked one of my sisters in the Lord if I could live with her until I got on my feet, and she turned me away.

Day and night, I was harassed by a spirit of fear and rejection tormenting my mind. I felt I had lost the closeness she and I had together. I didn't want to let her go; I had soul ties with Mrs. Beverely.

I felt that she was the only person who loved me, and now she is rejecting me like all the other people in my life have done. I knew that lust was attached to me, and this was the time I started masturbating with objects at night to satisfy my craving for her love.

Mrs. Beverely was in my heart like no other woman I had been with. Although it was hard to let her go, I had nowhere to run to. Many times, I felt like I was going to lose my mind again if I didn't get Mrs. Beverely out of my heart.

There was nothing I wouldn't do for Mrs. Beverely; she was aware of that. I believe she treated me the way she did because I was weak when it came down to her, and she knew it! I felt like I was just there because I served her at the time. I would shut myself in that little room, and no one knew the pain that was tearing me inside.

I began to realize that the way I was being treated was another form of abuse. And I was accustomed to abuse.

As time went by, I was looking for a way to break free from all this pain and torment. I felt so hopeless, and life had no meaning. Why am I still here? I even began to believe the lie that Satan told me in my mind that God is letting these things happen to you for all the wrong you have been doing.

Always putting others' needs before myself was a norm for me; making others happy, I felt that this was required of me. Many times, I did things just to be loved and accepted. I didn't realize that I, too, was using people in my own way.

Everything I gave, or when I served in these relationships with these women, I was looking for something in return: their love and acceptance. It was years before the soul ties that I had with Mrs. Beverely were broken.

Even when I finally broke free from under the same roof, in my mind, I was still bound to Mrs. Beverely. She went on with her life and never looked back at all the damage that she had caused in my life. After leaving and finally getting to my own place, there were still soul ties between us.

It was so hard to watch Mrs. Beverely go on with her life, and I was still stuck in a relationship all by myself. She never stops abusing me with her words. Many times, she would cut me so badly, and even when I told her that you really cut my heart, she would just look at me with her I don't care expression.

No one ever knew that I was overdosing myself with prescribed medicine right under their very nose. I just wanted the pain to stop; it was too much for me to bear.

Mrs. Beverely would sometimes pick me up to go with her somewhere. Everything would be going fine, and something I did or said would trigger her anger toward me again, and she would cut me so badly that I would hold my head down to the ground with tears rolling down my cheeks.

To say this made me sound crazy, but at the time, this was where my mind was. I poured everything I had in me into this relationship with Mrs. Beverely just for her to love me back. I almost lost my soul just to be with her.

Can you imagine loving someone like that and not receiving that same type of love back? Can you understand the depth of the love I had for Mrs. Beverely?

I used to wonder, when I was among the body of Christ if they could see my pain. Why would no one come to help me get out of this mess I put myself in? I would be so angry at myself for allowing the abuse that came my way.

I felt that I didn't have anyone to turn to, and the one person that I needed to turn to, I thought he was very angry at me for the things that I was doing, continually lying to God that I wasn't going to do this again, Lord.

The devil would have destroyed me in this relationship with Mrs. Beverely if he could have. I fell so deep in sin that when I used to feel convicted, I began to override the Holy Spirit, convicting me to stop.

My spirit was crying out for help. I want to be free. I was tired of giving out. The more I gave, the more people took from me.

A song I started writing and never finished, these two verses:

I gave so much of me, but I got so little in return.

Jesus, will You, would You, deliver me?

Chapter 15

A Plan of Assassination

I had finally come to the point at which I could not sleep at night. I either walked the floor all night, or I sat in the big chair in the living room. Not wanting to see daylight, I covered the window, so it stayed dark in my room most of the time.

One day, I was on my way to my cleaning business. Beverly was saying I had done some things that were not true. I don't know what happened after that. The mental stress from our conversation caused me to blackout. When that happened, I ran my car into a pole at a four-way stop sign. I did not want to live anymore. I was tired of the mental abuse.

I was taken to LBJ Hospital Emergency Hospital. My oldest sister, Mama, and Beverly were with me at the time. When the doctors came into the room with many questions, all I could do was cry.

A few weeks later, I was taken to the Ben Taub Hospital. Again, when the Doctor began asking me so many questions, all I could do was cry.

The Doctor told Beverly, "She is sick, but not one time has she asked for any medicine."

All I did was cry. I was so tired of the mental abuse from Beverly. All I had done was love her. Now, I just did not want to live anymore.

Beverly hated me and treated me as though I had no feelings. My family came to the hospital. I did not want to talk to them. I only wanted to talk to Beverly.

The next day, I returned to do my cleaning services in Houston. Suddenly, I began crying and shaking out of control. Beverly went to work that day with me. She called Pastor G. Jones who told her to take me to the hospital because I was having a nervous breakdown.

I told Beverly that I was not going to stay in a psychiatric ward. She told me that if I did not sign myself in, she was going to call Mama to come and sign me in to Harris County Psychiatric Ward. I signed myself into the ward.

I was in a room with another person. I did not sleep, eat, or talk to anyone. They finally prescribed some medicine so I could sleep. I still would not interact with anyone. I just slept. They wanted me to be a part of the group; I would not.

Beverly visited me just about every day. My family visited me once while I was in the psychiatric ward. They diagnosed me with manic depression and psychosis: I was hearing voices.

I stayed in the hospital for seven days. Beverly picked me up from the Psychiatric Ward. The medicine I was taking made me sleep all day and night.

Beverly went to the clinic where I was seeing a psychiatrist. She told them that all I did was sleep. They changed my medication schedule so I would take everything at night and be awake during the day.

I ended up back at Beverly's house. I felt I had lost everything: my business, my car, and myself. When I had the accident, two or three vehicles crashed because of me. God gave me favor; no one pressed charges.

Even though I went back to the House of God, I felt as though I was lost among all the Saints that were there with me.

During my entire time of being in relationships with people, it had never been about me. It has always centered around them: making them happy; giving them what they wanted. I learned that if you do not know who you are, others will continue to take and take and take from you. The only love I knew was to give, give, and give more. It was even hard for me to accept God's love.

In my mind, God was this Man upstairs. He was standing there, ready to beat me when I was bad. I could not actually accept that He really loved me. When I did something wrong, according to the Word of God, I felt as though He was rejecting me...like my parents.

I attended counseling three times every week. Sometimes, the counselor came to the house. At first, I was not there in the room with them. I was so withdrawn. Most of the time, I cried the entire time I was with the counselors.

I had never felt so unhappy and alone. I wondered how they could understand where I had been and what I had been through. Obviously, they had never experienced the things I had gone through in my life.

I am still a part of Ripley Clinic where I have been receiving counseling for over 20 years. I also still take depression and anxiety medicine.

As time went on, I began to open to my counselors. They asked about my relationship with Mama and Daddy. When I shared with them, I felt anger and bitterness. Tears rolled down my face.

I always blamed Daddy because I felt he was the beam that should have held everything together. When he left, our family did not have a leg to stand on.

They assigned another counselor to me. She instructed me to draw different pictures of my experiences.

After several more years, she left, and I was assigned to another counselor: Mrs. Blackwell. Mrs. Blackwell instructed me to draw pictures on how I was currently feeling in the moments we were together. During those moments, I felt angry, sad, alone, abandoned, and hurt.

I told her about Beverly and how she made me feel. I shared with Mrs. Blackwell that I had to get out of that house because Beverly did not care about me. She treated me like I was the cause of the things that happened in her life.

My last counselor was Judy Brown, a delivered lesbian who was saved and filled with the Holy Spirit. She lives in Humble. I met with her in the evenings at her office. She was a beautiful Woman of God, inside and out. She always started our sessions with prayer and the Word of God. Mrs. Brown's therapy took me to another level of deliverance.

I found Mrs. Brown very easy to talk to. Maybe it was because she could relate to some of the things I had been through. She asked me about Mama. Before she could finish with the question, I told her I hated Mama.

No! Not this Spirit-filled, Woman of God, full of hate and unforgiveness!

YES!

With the help of the Holy Spirit, Mrs. Brown pulled some things out of me that I didn't realize were in me.

She believed I had been molested as a child but had subconsciously hidden those memories in the back of my mind because they were so painful. I did not want to believe I had been molested as a child. She told me that all the signs were pointing to that occurring in my life.

I met with Mrs. Brown twice a week for three years. I was so happy to meet with her. She was able to reveal to me that I had low self-esteem and did not think much of myself.

She told me that I was allowing the devil to validate my worth through people. She let me know that the Word of God says that I was fearfully and wonderfully made and that there was no one else like me. She told me that I was the apple of God's eye, and that He loved me so much. She even told me that I must forgive my parents and all those who had hurt me if I wanted God to forgive me of my sins.

I told her, "I do not know how to do that."

She told me that the Spirit of the Living God would help me if I would be honest with Him.

I finally realized that being in Beverly's house was doing me more harm than good. Our relationship was no longer healthy for me. Even though I knew things weren't the same with us, I continued to share a soul-tie with Beverly. I discovered during this time that it is not easy to break away from soul-ties.

With Beverly, it seemed that the kinder I was to her, the worse she treated me. Even though the people of God could see the way I was being treated, no one came to my aid.

I began attending Lily of the Valley Apostolic Church. I shared my story with Pastor Brenda Jones about my previous lifestyle and how God had delivered me. She sat me down and would not let me do anything in ministry for a season. I was confused. I was not doing anything but trying to live holy, which was all I knew how to do. I was allowed to play the drums, but I was not allowed to teach Adult Sunday School.

I talked to God. I asked Him what I had done wrong. I wondered sometimes if my leader loved me. Sometimes, Pastor Brenda seemed to be so harsh with me. I was doing my best to please God and to please her as my leader.

One of the members of Lily of the Valley, Sister Gladys, allowed me to move in with her at Danville Apartments. Even though it wasn't very comfortable, I slept on the sofa. I never complained. I was just happy to be out of Beverly's house.

Sister Gladys and I seemed to be getting along very well. The only problem I had was when I brought my food using my food stamps: she would sometimes eat up the things I liked without asking me. I never said anything about it to her because I was in her house; I didn't want to make waves.

One Wednesday night at Bible Study, we were all at the altar praying. I was pouring out my heart to God.

Pastor Brenda touched me and said, "Zeal."

Because I did not know what that meant, I lost my focus. After Bible Study was over, I went over to the table where Pastor Brenda sat.

I said, "Pastor Jones, I am not trying to receive what God has said through you, but what do you mean by *zeal*?

As she walked toward the entrance, she said I was all over the place, and she must calm me down. When I left the house of God that night, I went home and researched the word *zeal* in the dictionary. I read the meaning. There was nothing bad about *zeal* in the dictionary. I researched the Word of God in the Concordance in the back of my Bible. I couldn't find anything bad about *zeal*. The definition of *zealous* was enthusiastic and eager. (Cambridge Dictionary)

I even found a scripture that Jesus was *zealous* for God: the *zeal* of Jesus, our Great Example.

John 2:17 KJV *The zeal of thine house hath eaten me up.*

When Jesus arrived in Jerusalem, the city was crowded with people. They had come to celebrate Passover. He went to the temple and saw the merchants and money changers. They were selling oxen, sheep, and doves to be used as sacrifices. Jesus saw the money changers doing business and making profits within the temple court. He made a whip and drove them out.

John 2:16 – 17 KJV *And said unto them that sold doves, Take these things hence; make not my Father's house an house of merchandise. And his disciples remembered that it was written, The zeal of thine house hath eaten me up.*

This can be translated, "Zeal for Thy house consumes me." The Greek word translated *zeal* means *fervor*. It is from the root word that means, 'to be hot, earnest, fervent.'

The Bible says that Christ left *us an example, that ye should follow his steps.* **(See 1 Peter 2:21)**

Jesus was *zealous*, earnest, hot, and fervent for the honor of God's house. We should follow His example.

We should be *zealous*, earnest, hot, and fervent for the house of God which is the Church of the Living God. **(See 1 Timothy 3:15)**

We should be *zealous* of good works in the church of the Living God. **(See Titus 2:14)**

So, I wondered to myself what was wrong with me being *zealous* for the Lord. I had been excited about the Lord and the work of the Lord since I had given my life to Jesus. Now someone was telling me they must *calm me down.*

That next Sunday service, I just sat there. I said to myself that if this was what Pastor Brenda wanted me to do, then this was what I was going to do. I would not clap my hands, sing, or move.

Pastor Brenda and her daughter, Co-Pastor Linda Wood, watched me. I felt that she was asking me to die. Ever since I had been in Jesus, I was excited for the Lord. Now, something was wrong with me.

I was told that the only way I was going to know the voice of God was through Pastor Brenda Jones.

So, everything within me was trying to receive what God was speaking through Pastor Brenda. I was wrestling in my spirit not to receive what God was saying to me.

The next Wednesday, we had Bible Study again. Different Saints were getting up and sharing their testimonies. I finally stood up to testify.

I said, "Hallelujah!"

The Saints responded back with a *Hallelujah*.

I thanked God for my leader speaking to me about *zeal* and I received it in the name of the Lord. I thanked God for my life and how He saved me and filled me with His Holy Spirit.

After I sat down, Pastor Brenda stood up and said, "No. You did not receive what I said."

I could not deny that she was telling the truth. I was struggling with the words she gave me. My spirit just could not agree with what she had told me. I wasn't given clarity on what Pastor Brenda was saying to me. I left that night with my head hanging down. I felt like God was saying I had something bad. I couldn't shake what Pastor Brenda had spoken over me concerning *zeal*.

In that same week, on Sunday morning for Sunday School, Evangelist Janet was teaching the lesson.

Evangelist Lois and Evangelist Dangerfield were participating in the Sunday School class for the day. As I listened to the teachers, I had a question. I raised my hand. Sister Janet acknowledged my hand and allowed me to ask the question.

When I asked the question, none of the ministers there could answer my question. Because the teacher could not answer the question and none of the other ministers could answer the question, pride stood up. They began calling me the devil.

Evangelist Lois told Evangelist Janet to pray against the devil. Evangelist Janet began praying. I guess I was the devil they were praying against. I was shocked that Evangelist Lois would say I was the devil.

On that same Sunday during our evening service, Evangelist Janet and Evangelist Berta were serving as Pastor Brenda's Armor-bearers. They shared what had happened in Sunday School when the service began. Pastor Brenda rebuked me from the pulpit as a result of what she was told by her Armor-bearers.

I was hurt. Pastor Brenda had only heard one side of the story. Our guest speaker for the service was Pastor Darlene. She preached on *zeal* and the *zeal* of Jesus. I held back my tears. The Praise Team sang some praise songs. Afterward, it was time for our guest speaker to bring the Word of God.

Pastor Darlene stood up and exhorted for a few minutes. She opened her Bible and gave us the scriptures. The subject she was going to preach was...*Zeal*. I knew God didn't want me to be confused as to what He was saying to me. God sent a message to me that I had done nothing wrong and my *zeal* for Him was pleasing in His sight.

I praised God until I was tired. I thanked God that He would not allow anyone to change who I am in Him. God used Pastor Darlene to encourage my heart that day. Unfortunately, I still couldn't let go of what Pastor Brenda had sown into my heart.

I feel that if she had sat me down and explained what God was saying, I could have gotten a better understanding. Just leaving me wondering what God was saying to me was wrong in my eyes.

Many times, I felt that Pastor Brenda didn't like me; I didn't know why. Sometimes, I felt like I was dealing with two people.

One time when Pastor Brenda was sitting down in the fellowship hall eating, I sat down beside her. I began sharing with her that I could see in the service that the Spirit of God was not moving and something was wrong.

Pastor Brenda said, "That was discernment."

I asked her if she could teach me how to discern. She said she couldn't teach me how to discern, but she could teach me how to pray. She said she would get with me, to just give her a few days.

Time went by. I was so excited that my leader was going to teach me to pray. Weeks and months went by. Pastor Brenda never got with me. One day, I texted Pastor Brenda and told her I was ready and waiting for her to teach me to pray.

Pastor Brenda texted me and rebuked me from my head to my toes. I never knew the reason why.

I cried out to the Lord, asking, "Father, why is she treating me the way she does?"

I honestly wondered sometimes if I was dealing with two people or not. I wanted so much to be the one God would use to show Pastor Brenda that her labor was not in vain.

Many of those whose lives she had sown into had gone forward in their own ministries. Those same ones did not allow her to be their covering. I wanted the Lord to let me be one He would raise in ministry and Pastor Brenda would be my covering.

On a Saturday evening, Pastor Brenda called a meeting with the ministers of the church. Pastor was going over the pamphlet she had created about the vision and belief of the ministry. She shared with us that it was time to get out and work to build the ministry. She shared that we should get out and win souls for Christ.

In my mind, I was screaming, "YES!" This was what Jesus had taught His disciples about Kingdom work.

After that meeting, I was very excited! I went home and started praying, asking God what I could do to help the ministry. I always believed, and still do believe, that the work of the Kingdom is not so much inside the building, but in the highways and hedges – the streets.

I was searching the internet, also. The thought came to me about a prison ministry. I researched on the internet about prison ministry.

That's how I became connected to Sister Darlene Jackson.

Sister Jackson was well known by city officials. She had organized a prison ministry that had been very successful for over 20 years.

Her phone number was on her website with the prison ministry information and her pictures. I decided to give her a call to see if she could help me organize a prison ministry in the ministry I was attending.

I connected with her and introduced myself. I shared what was on my heart about starting a prison ministry at our church. Sister Jackson shared about how God had started her in prison ministry. I was on Cloud Nine.

She asked if I could come to the meeting they were having on Saturday afternoon. I asked her to let me get with my Pastor to see if it would be alright for me to attend.

I excitedly called Pastor Brenda, telling her everything Sister Jackson had shared with me. I asked if it would be alright for me to attend the Saturday meeting. She gave me permission.

I could hardly wait for Saturday to come. I was with Beverly that Saturday morning before the meeting. As happened so often, she got into her flesh, and I followed along with her in my flesh. I hated the way I allowed her to make me feel after I left her presence. I was either angry or maybe just hurt that she would treat me the way she often did.

I went to the meeting with my chin up. I was not going to let Sister Beverly discourage me on this exciting day. She dropped me off at the meeting location at 5021 Hillside Dr. Road at the Plaza Conference Building.

I went in. Most of the Saints were already seated. I sat down by one of the sisters. Sister Jackson opened the meeting by sharing the many things that were coming up for the prison ministry.

Sister Jackson introduced me to everyone as Sister Carla. I gave a pleasant smile and said I was glad to be there. Everyone said they were glad to have me there. Sister Jackson continued the meeting.

After Sister Jackson gave the information on what was going to take place over the following months, she shared that most of those at the meeting had previously been prison inmates who had all given their lives to Jesus Christ. Now, though, they were in ministry for themselves. They had joined Sister Jackson and were offering their service to the Lord by ministering to other inmates.

When the meeting was over, I interacted with Sister Jackson and the people of God. Sister Jackson let me know that Sister Tasha Love would get with me and send me all the information I needed to share with my Pastor the following week.

Sister Love and I exchanged phone numbers. She told me she would call me the following Monday. I left the meeting feeling like I had a purpose in ministry. I was so excited. I couldn't wait to share the information with Pastor Brenda.

When I got home, I texted Pastor Brenda to let her know I would have the information to share with her the following week.

She texted back, "OK, Sister Carla."

Time went on. I had not received the information from Sister Love. I was feeling anxious because I wanted to get the information to my Pastor as soon as possible so we could start the prison ministry. Sister Love called to tell me she had mailed the information I needed to start a prison ministry connected with Sister Jackson.

I received the information that Wednesday afternoon. I was excited I could finally get the information to Pastor Brenda, and we could move forward with the prison ministry.

I texted Pastor and let her know I had the information. I asked when we could get together. I wasn't expecting Pastor Brenda to respond the way she did. She rebuked me and told me she had to harness the spirit I had. When I read the text, tears rolled down my cheeks.

I questioned in my mind, "*What just happened here? What did I do wrong?*"

I was confused. We never spoke about this situation again. Once again, I held the hurt and pain inside of myself from trying to do something good.

That Sunday morning, I refused to move. People were praising God.

I said to myself, "If this is what you want me to do, then I want to do nothing."

I wouldn't clap my hand during the singing with the Body of Christ. I was hurt and angry with Pastor Brenda. She had led me to believe I was doing a good thing and she was pleased. I watched them as they watched me. I vowed not to move an inch.

Thank God that in His mercy, He spared my life in my foolishness. I wasn't harming anyone but myself. This spirit was an extension of rejection.

I talked to myself in my mind, "What are you doing? You have been a different person since you gave your life to Jesus Christ. You have been excited about the things of God. Now, why are you letting the enemy take that away from you?"

I took my eyes off the people and repented within myself. Tears rolled down my face. I asked God for forgiveness because He had done no wrong to me.

I began giving my Father what was due to Him: all the praise in Jesus' name! That spirit had to leave me alone. I learned throughout my Christian walk that if you are going to get delivered, it's going to be among your brothers and sisters in the Lord. Because we have a way of bringing out the best or the worst in each other, I believe God designed deliverance to come in this way.

Sister Bobbie Henderson, another member of Lily of the Valley, extended the love of Christ to me by opening her home to me. She and I were friends and co-workers. She and her sister Darlene used to work for me in my cleaning service. Sister Bobbie was so good to me. She kept some children in her home, also. The room I slept in was where the children usually play and take their naps.

I was very grateful to Sister Bobbie for making that sacrifice for me. Sister Bobbie was straight up with me when she knew I was wrong, even when I was right. I would talk to her with many tears about the hurts and pain I felt inside. I would even talk about Pastor Brenda with her, asking her why the Pastor didn't like me.

Sister Bobbie told me, "Pastor thinks very highly of you. She loves you."

She even told me that the mantle of Pastor Brenda should have fallen on me.

I then asked her, "Why does she keep treating me the way she does? She often tells me that I must stop letting the devil talk to my mind."

There were many Wednesdays and Sundays when I would come home to Sister Bobbie's home and cry in my room. I didn't understand Pastor Brenda and the way she handled me as a sheep.

There was nothing Sister Bobbie had that she did not share with me. She wasn't only my sister in Christ, Sister Bobbie was my friend. When I was disturbed about things, Sister Bobbie would give me the Word of God and encourage me in the Lord. She always knew when I was dealing with depression on another level. I always felt peace at Sister Bobbie's house. Sister Bobbie helped me so much during those hurtful times. She knew what was going on in my past.

I asked Sister Bobbie, "Why won't Pastor Brenda talk to me directly? Why is she always sending messages to me through Sister Beverly?"

That really did not sit right with me. I felt that people never deliver messages the way a person gives the message; especially when the message sometimes causes me to get angry.

Chapter 16

Lord, Why Me?

On a Saturday evening in 2009, Sister Lulu, Sister Gladys, Sister Karen, and I decided to go and clean the church. We all rode with Sister Karen to Lily of the Valley Apostolic Church. Sister Gladys and Sister Karen were having some disagreement about who was cleaning where.

I tried to help the situation by saying, "Why don't you all work together and I will work by myself?"

They all seemed to agree with that plan. As time went on, I was cleaning Pastor Brenda's office. Sister Lulu came in while I was finishing up dusting the furniture. Sister Lulu said that she didn't mind helping me clean.

I replied to Sister Lulu that I appreciated her. I didn't know that Lulu had come in to give me a message from her sister Karen that Karen was ready to go because she had other things to do. I finished Pastor Brenda's bathroom. We left the office as I turned the lights off.

When I went to the front of the Sanctuary, Sister Karen was upset that I was just coming out. I did not know that her sister had not given me the message.

I apologized to Sister Karen. "I'm sorry. I didn't know. I'm riding with you. And if you are ready to go, I must leave with you."

She was my ride home. I turned off all the lights in the entrance, locked the doors, got in the car, and we left.

I did not find out until later, after I moved back to Houston, that Sister Gladys went to Sister Dora and told her that Sister Karen wanted to leave that day because she had something to do but I kept on cleaning. Sister Dora told Co-Pastor Linda. Co-Pastor Linda called Sister Gladys, Sister Lula, and Sister Karen and talked to them without me being present. They shared what had happened that Saturday at the church. Co-Pastor Linda had only one side of the story.

At the church on Friday night, we had marriage enrichment. Pastor Brenda allowed the singles to attend that night. Co-Pastor Linda taught that night. Everyone asked different questions. Sister Kathy asked Co-Pastor Linda a question concerning marriage. She answered her question.

My hand had been raised for a few minutes. I believe she had intentionally ignored my raised hand. Co-Pastor Linda finally acknowledged I had been holding up my hand for a long time.

I stood up and said, "Co-Pastor Wood, what does the word *zeal* mean?"

Co-Pastor Wood answered me in such a harsh way. I didn't know that Co-Pastor Wood went to Sister Karen, Sister Lula, and Sister Gladys about the cleaning we all had done on that Saturday evening.

She said I was trying to come at people with the Word of God to do what I wanted it to do. "Everyone is not into cleaning like you. You want to know the opposite of *zeal?* It is *fanatic?* You are a fanatic."

I did everything I could to hold back the tears.

Sister Kathy came to me and said, "Do not take this in a bad way."

I asked her how else I could take it and walked out of the church. I sat in the car, tears rolling down my face.

I could not believe what had just happened in that building. Sister Beverly came to the car. I was crying, but she did not really care that I was having an anxiety attack. She asked if I needed her to take me to the hospital. I told her no.

She drove me home. She neither tried to encourage nor console me. She just let me sit there in the car, hurt and crying. I went into the house to my room. I decided I was going to move to Tulsa, Oklahoma with my dad.

Sister Beverly took my decision to move to Tulsa to Pastor Brenda. She said it would be a good idea for me.

Sister Dora said to me, "Now, Sister Beverly doesn't have to deal with you anymore."

I knew at that point that there had been some talking going on concerning me.

The reason I moved to Tulsa was for two reasons. First, I was tired of the way Beverly treated me. Secondly, I was also very angry for whatever lies Sister Karen, Sister Lula, and Sister Gladys had told that caused Co-Pastor Wood to snap at me the way she had done in the marriage enrichment class. I was tired of feeling like my Pastor had two personalities and didn't care much for me.

I now realize that I allowed the enemy to blind me to a lot of things that were good that took place at Lily of the Valley Apostolic Church. I now realize that what the enemy meant for my harm, God turned it around for my good. There was a lot of growing up I needed to do.

Because of Pastor Jones, I matured in so many areas of my life. Spiritually, mentally, and emotionally, there were things that needed to take place inside of me before God could bring forth the ministry He had called me to. I don't believe I would be totally delivered today if it had not been for the ministry of Lily of the Valley and Pastor Brenda Jones.

Pastor Jones is a woman of much faith. God has given her the eyes of an eagle. She is a woman that is given to much prayer and the Word of God. She taught me to stand up for myself in many ways because I was very timid.

There was not one member under her leadership in which God didn't reveal their strengths and weaknesses. Pastor Jones not only taught me, but she also led by example. She brought me to a higher level in prayer. For that, I want to say, "**Thank you!**"

Everything I experienced in the ministry of Lily of the Valley caused me to grow up in many areas of my life. I share my experiences about what I went through in the Body of Christ because I need to let others know that whatever they are dealing with, whether similar to or the same as I experienced, it is for their growth in the Lord.

God knew I didn't need a leader to pamper me through the process of my complete deliverance. To be honest, that's what I expected Pastor Jones to do. I am sure God revealed that to her. My desire for Pastor Jones was to take me under her arms. Part of me was disappointed when she didn't.

I truly admire Pastor Jones in the Holy Ghost. I admire most of all, though, her prayer life that she showed me in the Lord. I didn't realize until one December that I had held unforgiveness in my heart against Pastor Jones.

And so, I made up my mind to move to Tulsa. Even though she had treated me badly over those few years, Sister Beverly didn't want me to leave. Unfortunately, I was still in love with her. It took me two weeks before I was able to let go of what we did not have anymore and move.

Chapter 17

This Was My Heart!

At the end of November 2008, I moved to Tulsa to be with my Dad. For a few months, I did not attend church.

Dad owned his own business. I got up every morning and fixed his breakfast and lunch for the day. While he was gone, I cleaned the house because his house was a mess. When Dad came home from work, I always had a hot dinner prepared for him.

When I finished getting his house in order, it looked like a different home. Daddy would go on about his religion and get mad at me when I used the Bible to shoot down his beliefs. He would go into his room, call Lois on the phone, and talk about me to her.

I had been in Tulsa for about two weeks. One morning, Daddy knocked on my door and told me he had some bad news. I could tell he was having a hard time telling me the news.

I asked, "Daddy, what is wrong?"

He said, "Carl passed."

I said, "What did you say?"

He responded, "Carla, Carl passed this morning."

My legs got weak. I began to cry. I could not stop crying. Daddy tried to console me.

All I could say, over and over, was, "I told him to come with me so I could take care of him. Daddy, I told him. But he wanted to come later."

I had tried to persuade my twin to come to Tulsa with me when I moved. He told me he would come later. All Carl wanted was to be with his family. They told me that before Carl died, God granted his petition.

That day, I cried all day into the evening. Daddy did not know how to console me. I did not want to be consoled. I wanted my twin brother Carl. He and I had a bond that could not be broken.

Most of my crying was from me blaming myself for Carl's death. I believed that if I had stayed in Texas, Carl would be alive today. I blamed myself for Carl's death; especially when I found out how he died. Carl had lain in his apartment for about three or four days before anyone knew he was dead.

This really caused me to blame myself for his death. Had I been there, I would have called and checked on him every day. I would have known whether he was sick or not. When Carl did not show up for dialysis, the dialysis center called Mama to find out why Carl had not shown up.

Mama had our little sister, Princess, take her over to Carl's apartment to see what was going on with him. When they arrived, Carl did not answer the door. They went to the leasing office and told them what was going on.

The office staff got a key, and they went with Mama and Princess to Carl's apartment. When they got there, they found Carl dead on the floor.

It did not matter what Carl had done in his life; he was my twin. I loved him with my soul. I did not think I could go on without him. Although Carl was involved in many bad things, when he called and needed me, I made my way to him. Carl was my heart. Unfortunately, the things Carl did caused much danger in his life.

Carl was headstrong. Once Carl got something in his mind, it was hard to change. I am just like my twin in that way.

Carl was in the prison system as a teenager. Even in prison, Carl had to deal with how to survive. So many times, he got into fights that almost cost him his life. Carl had many near-death experiences from prison and on to the streets of Barrett Station.

Many times, we received calls that Carl was in the hospital. They did not think Carl was going to pull through. But God... In His mercy, God spared Carl's life many times.

When Daddy left Texas to move to Tulsa, Carl dropped out of school and hooked up with our cousin, Mark. Mark was a drug dealer. Carl not only sold drugs, he also became addicted to the drugs he was around. As a teenager, when Carl was released from prison, he always had a car or motorcycle or something to get around with. He also always had money in his pockets. I never understood how he could have access to the things he had. I believe Carl was in some deep stuff.

One year, Mama called Daddy and asked if he could take Carl to stay with him. Carl moved to Tulsa; that stay did not last long: Carl messed with Daddy's girlfriend. Daddy sent him back to Texas so he would not kill Carl. Once back in Barrett Station, Carl resumed his old life, landing him back in prison because of drugs.

I cried when I saw him being released from prison. He looked like the Incredible Hulk. After a week or two, he returned to his cocaine habit. Before long, Carl began to look more like Peewee Herman. In prison, they called Carl *Preacher*. In the streets, they called him *Brown Cow*.

When Carl became ill, the first person he called was his twin sister. Carl knew that whatever it took, I was going to get to him. It was very hard to see and watch Carl destroy his life with cocaine. He seemed to not be able to leave that *white girl* alone. That is what they call cocaine in the streets – **White Girl**.

I witnessed what cocaine was doing to my twin brother. Cocaine was eating Carl inside and out. It was hard for me to deal with many times; he was such a part of me. I could not ignore the bond we had.

When Carl first got out of prison, I started buying clothes and other things he needed for him. I put money in Carl's pockets because he was a man; I knew there were times when he wanted to go to the store and get a few things on his own. I dressed him and gave him money every week...until I discovered he still had a problem with drugs.

After being in prison for 21 years, Carl had never had a birthday party. I gave him a birthday party.

Sometimes, Carl would come up missing: I would go looking for him. One time, I found him sleeping outside of a carwash. Another time, I found him sleeping under a bridge. Those times I found him; he would be very dirty. Cocaine caused his skin to turn darker than usual. He had lost so much weight; he was small.

Carl had many health problems. When he was on drugs, he did not take care of himself. I told him that he was going to come and live with me. The places Carl had previously lived were very nice places. But because he had spent most of his life in prison, Carl did not know how to adjust to rules.

While serving his time, Carl received much book knowledge. That book knowledge made it hard for anyone to be able to tell him anything. He knew the law backwards and forwards. Carl knew the Bible from Genesis to Revelation. He knew the Bible better than I did.

Carl fell in love with a young lady named Tony. I thought and hoped this connection would turn his life around.

Sister Tony had two children: Taylor and Lucas. They loved Carl like he was their real daddy. Tony was a Christian woman, and Carl treated her with respect. Unfortunately, Carl could not beat the cocaine habit. I believe Sister Tony loved Carl. Sadly, she could not deal with his cocaine habit.

In 2007, I was still living with Sister Beverly. She was a cousin on my Dad's side of the family. Before we knew we were related, we were in a relationship.

I received a call from Mama to tell me they had rushed Carl to the hospital. Beverly drove me to San Jacinto Hospital in Baytown, Texas.

When we arrived at the hospital, we could not see Carl right away. They took us into a small room to wait on the doctor. The Doctor came to us about 20 minutes after we arrived.

He introduced himself. "Hi. I am Doctor Dove."

He sat down and shared that he did not know if Mr. Williams was going to make it through the night. I cried so hard; my cries became loud. I could not control the tears falling on my cheeks.

I began to pray, "No, Lord. My brother cannot die. I cannot make it without my twin brother, Carl."

Dr. Dove said I could go to Carl's room. When I went to his room, I could not believe all the machines hooked to him. He was in a coma. I cried and prayed again that the Lord would spare his life. We had been this way many times; God had spared his life before.

I used to think Carl had nine lives...like a cat. Carl came through; God brought him through. He came out of that coma. Now, though, he had other problems. Doctor Dove discovered that Carl had cancer and kidney failure. Carl had to be put on dialysis.

Carl also had other underlying problems: diabetes, high blood pressure, HIV, seizures, and some other health problems I can't recall. For a short time, he came to live with me. It was not easy, though, because I couldn't tell Carl anything: he knew everything! Although he had a lot of book knowledge, Carl did not have much common sense.

Because of his attitude and because he would stick his nose where it did not belong, Carl had been taken out of many of the places in which he had lived.

At one time, I was looking for Carl on the streets of Houston in the drug areas. I did not know Carl had changed his name. On the streets, he was known as *Curtis*. Even though these places in which I searched for my brother were not places for me to be, I did not care. This was my twin brother. I needed to know if he was alright.

The men and women in the places I went to in my search for my brother were also on drugs. On the streets, drug addicts look out for each other. When I showed pictures of Carl, and asked if anyone had seen him, they never pointed me towards my brother. Even though they knew the face in the picture, and they knew his street name, they never turned Carl in to me. However, they got word from him that his twin sister was showing his picture around and asking about his whereabouts.

Eventually, Carl would come to the surface. He was not happy that I was showing his picture on the streets. Because of the deep things Carl was involved in from his past, I believe he became paranoid. He was always looking over his shoulders.

When we were told that Carl had passed, Daddy flew me back to Texas first. I arrived Friday morning. Sister Beverly picked me up from the airport and took me to her house in McNair. I could not hold back the tears when I got into the car with her.

Mama told Sister Beverly that they did not want me to view the body before the funeral. Mama had already seen Carl's body when they found him dead in his apartment.

She did not want me to see his deformed face. Carl had lain on his face for four days. His face was smashed from lying on the floor for so long. Although I did not know he did not look like himself, I was determined to view his body.

My family was at the funeral home when I arrived. I had walked halfway down the aisle toward Carl's coffin. When I finally saw him, I turned around and ran out of the funeral home screaming, "That is not my brother! That is not my brother! I want my brother! That is not my brother!"

I ran into the road, screaming and hollering, "That is not my brother!"

My cousin caught up with me and grabbed me, pulling me out of the road.

Sister Beverly tried to calm me down. She did not help; she only made it worse by screaming at me. Mama came and calmed me down. They gave me a pill so I could sleep. I cried until the pill put me to sleep.

I was able to handle Carl's funeral only by the grace of God. On the day of the funeral, I did not cry at all. It wouldn't be until later when I realized I hadn't grieved for my brother.

One night, in the middle of the night in my apartment, I was on my keyboard. In my mind and heart, I could hear the music and words to a song about Carl. I grabbed a piece of paper to write the words down so I could put music to the song. I put the music to the words for this song:

I love you so much; there's an empty place in my heart today.

I never had the chance; never had the chance.

I never had the chance to say goodbye.

Carl, I miss you so, my prayer is that you made it home.

I never had the chance; never had the chance.

I never had the chance to say goodbye.

As I played and sang this song, deep in the gut of my heart, I felt the loss of my twin brother, Carl. I cried so hard until I was soaking wet from the pain I felt.

I realized then that I had never grieved for the loss of my twin brother, Carl Antony Williams. I had to allow myself to go through the grieving process.

Chapter 18

Out of the Frying Pan into the Fire

When I moved to Tulsa, I was very angry at some of the people in the house of God. It was some months before I started attending a place of worship.

During this time, Daddy talked about Miss Gloria Hudson. She was an African American woman who owned her own school: The Gloria Hudson Academy School. Miss Gloria's school is rated the number one school in Tulsa.

If this lady liked Daddy, I would be glad for him. I just did not want to see him being used. Daddy had a small picture of Miss Gloria on his dining room wall. He told me she was not an ordinary lady: she was a classic, smart, beautiful, and intelligent woman.

At some point, Daddy did some work for Miss Gloria at her home. He would also buy Miss Gloria the special kind of drink she liked. He was trying to establish a relationship with her because he really liked her.

Daddy gave me the job of ordering the different things Miss Gloria liked. I finally told Daddy he needed to stop buying Miss Gloria things until he found out how she felt about him. He paid no attention to me and continued ordering the things she liked.

I ordered four cases of the juices she liked. Several days before Thanksgiving, Daddy called Miss Gloria to let her know he was going to have a turkey fried for her.

Don't get me wrong: I wanted Daddy to have someone. I wanted him to be able to be with someone, because every night, he would come into my room and talk for a long time. Then, he would fall asleep. I knew he needed someone in his life he could talk to; someone he could establish a relationship with outside of me.

When Daddy fell asleep while he supposedly talked to me in the evenings, I would tell him, "Daddy, wake up and go to bed."

Over and over, he would tell me that he was not asleep.

Before I met Miss Gloria, Daddy took me to get my nails done at Polly Nail Shop. There, I met a woman named Carla Brown. While I got my nails done, Daddy slept outside in the car. I told Carla about Daddy. I wanted to introduce them. I told her that Daddy was very nice, and single.

I went outside to get Daddy and invited him into the nail shop. I introduced them. They began talking. When Carla finished with my nails, she and Daddy exchanged numbers.

I was glad they hit it off. Not just because I was tired of Daddy sitting up half the night talking to me and falling asleep, though. Now, Daddy would have a woman to talk to and be with. That relationship only lasted about a month. Daddy tried to enforce his religious beliefs on Carla. They had one date. Afterward, Carla told Daddy she would call when she was ready.

Daddy decided he was going to show up on her doorstep. I don't know why he did that. This angered Carla. Carla stopped answering his calls. When that happened, he started talking more to me again. I asked him how Carla was doing. He told me Carla would not answer his calls.

I said, "Daddy, I bet you keep trying to force your religion on Carla."

I wanted to get in touch with Carla to find out what had happened, but I did not know how. But I must tell you: God does work in mysterious ways.

One day, to my surprise when I was in Wal-Mart, I saw Carla in line at the checkout counter. We talked for a good while. She told me what Daddy had done to cause her to stop answering his calls. She said she was tired of hearing about his religion. I did not know what to do with that.

When I eventually moved into my own place, Daddy said I had moved where the white people lived...until he discovered that Carla lived on the same street. When he discovered this fact, he excused me for moving to Jansen Street because of the benefit of being closer to Carla.

On Thanksgiving Day, Daddy called Miss Gloria to tell her he was bringing the turkey. She invited us to eat Thanksgiving dinner with her and her family.

Miss Gloria lived on the other side of Tulsa; the side where people had money. We drove to her house, and Daddy proudly carried the turkey to her door. I knocked on the door. Miss Gloria answered the door; we went inside.

At first, I was a little withdrawn; I did not know Miss Gloria and her family. She asked me how long I had been in Tulsa. I told her I had been there for just a month.

While we were all talking and laughing, as usual, Daddy fell asleep in the big chair he was sitting on. Miss Gloria, her brother, Peter, and his girlfriend, Jane, were all laughing and talking while Daddy slept in the chair.

Miss Gloria's daughter, Brook, came in with her big dog. That dog was almost taller than me! Miss Gloria introduced me to Brook. Although Brook's dog was not a mean dog, he did not take very well to strangers.

I can't remember what Miss Gloria needed from the store, but Daddy volunteered to go to the store for her. Miss Gloria and I hit it off quickly. When Daddy came back, we were all just laughing and having a good time. Miss Gloria warmed up the food and fixed plates for Daddy and me. We sat down and ate. The hour was late, so Miss Gloria also fixed some food for us to take home with us.

Miss Gloria gave me her phone number. She told me that if I wanted to call her, I could. Daddy did not know I had her phone number; I kept that to myself. The next day, I woke up and fixed Daddy his breakfast and lunch to take to work with him. Afterward, I made my bed, took a bath, cleaned the house, and started dinner.

I called Miss Gloria. There was something about her that pulled me toward her. I knew that feeling all too well. I told Miss Gloria my whole life history.

I shared with her that I had been in several lesbian relationships. Why did I share all these things with a perfect stranger? I can't answer that question.

I believe the spirit of lust in me was drawn to the spirit of lust in Miss Gloria. I believe this is where the attraction came from. I was drawn by this spirit. After I told Miss Gloria about my lifestyle, she began testing me.

Miss Gloria had a cleaning lady, Demetria, who had been cleaning Miss Gloria's house for over 5 years. She told me that Demetria was a little masculine. I was at her house one day and met Demetria. I picked up on the fact that Demetria did not like that Miss Gloria and I were friends.

Miss Gloria and I were as different as night and day when it came to religious beliefs, though. She was Jehovah's Witness; I was Apostolic. She would tell me that what I believed was wrong and that her religion was the true religion.

The darkness has nothing to do with the light or vice versa. They do not mix. What happens when a room is totally dark, and you add light? The darkness disappears. What happens when there is a light in the room, and you add darkness? The darkness again disappears! Darkness cannot stand before light. Deception cannot stand before the truth! If we have God's Words, and we shine them on falsehood, the errors become glaring.

St. John 1:5 *And the light shines in the darkness and the darkness did not comprehend it.*

I knew I should not have befriended Gloria. She was in a cult and was being taught heresy. She was not a Christian; she did the things of the world. I knew the history of the Jehovah's Witness. Unfortunately, I still ignored all the warning signs to please my flesh.

Romans 7:18 AMP *For I know that nothing good lives in me, that is, in my flesh [my human nature, my worldliness – my sinful capacity]. For the willingness [to do good] is present in me, but the doing of good is not.*

2 Corinthians 6:14 – 18 AMPC [14]*Do not be unequally yoked with unbelievers [do not make mismatched alliances with them or come under a different yoke with them, inconsistent with your faith]. For what partnership has right living and right standing with God with iniquity and lawlessness? Or how can light have fellowship with darkness?*

[15]*What harmony can there be between Christ and Belial [the devil]? Or what has a believer in common with an unbeliever?*

[16]*What agreement [can there be between] a temple of God and idols? For we are the temple of the living God; even as God said, I will dwell in and with and among them and will walk in and with and among them, and I will be their God, and they shall be My people.*

[17]*So, come out from among [unbelievers], and separate (sever) yourselves from them, says the Lord, and touch not [any] unclean*

thing; then I will receive you kindly and treat you with favor,

[18]*And I will be a Father to you, and you shall be My sons and daughters, says the Lord Almighty.*

I began working for Miss Gloria at her Academy. I helped sometimes with teaching some of her classes and with teaching music to the students.

I also began spending nights at Miss Gloria's big home. Although I knew what I was doing was wrong, I began desiring Miss Gloria in an unnatural way. She was very much aware of how I felt.

I started staying away from Daddy's house for weeks at a time. One day, I asked Gloria if she would mind taking me to Daddy's house to get some more clothes. Miss Gloria had never stepped foot into Daddy's home until that day. The day Daddy saw Miss Gloria coming into his house with me, our relationship changed. Daddy stopped talking to me.

He told my Cousin Beverly that I had done to him the same thing my twin brother had done by sleeping with his former girlfriend, Peggie. As I was getting my clothes to take with me to Miss Gloria's house, Daddy and Miss Gloria made some small talk.

I entered the room and told Daddy I would see him later. Miss Gloria and I left the house, got into the car, and drove off. Daddy watched us leave.

Miss Gloria is a very elegant woman who lives in a fine house. She had fine clothes and money. Unfortunately, she also used profanity a lot. At that time, I was turned off to profanity; I did not use it.

When you begin walking in your flesh, though, you will find yourself compromising your standards of holiness. Even though I did not use profanity at the time, the more time I spent with Miss Gloria, I started saying a few choice words here and there.

I began driving Miss Gloria's expensive sports car. She began taking good care of me. I signed up for a jewelry account to buy Miss Gloria expensive pearl sets and diamond necklaces. One time, I used Daddy's credit card without his knowledge to buy something for Miss Gloria. When he found out, I told him I had bought a diamond ring for myself. He was still angry, though, because that was not what I was supposed to use his credit card for.

Now, let me just say this: Miss Gloria did not need those things. She had everything a woman needed or wanted. She had the money to buy those things for herself. I just wanted to please her because I was really falling for her.

I signed up for Section Eight. Things had changed between Daddy and me because of my relationship with Gloria. Finally, the Section Eight people called me. I moved to Little Creek Apartments.

I had not gone to church for a while. My spirit was convicted, so I decided to find a ministry. I started visiting Lily Full Gospel Church. My stay was not long with them. It was not the sisters who made me feel welcome; it was all the men in the church.

Even though that was strange to me, the women of the church were very standoffish to me. They were very jealous sisters. I went a couple of times more. Then, I just stopped going. I did not like how the women of the church treated me; I had done nothing for them to act this way.

I finally found a ministry I could call home. I joined St. Paul Holiness Church under the leadership of Pastor Betty Howard. Pastor Howard did not make me feel comfortable being there, though. I tried to overlook what I felt from her.

I realized I needed the strength of the Body of Christ if I was going to come out of what I was doing. I joined the choir and became one of the lead singers. Although I was faithful to the ministry, I was not faithful in heart like I normally would have been. I wanted to talk to someone. Unfortunately, I did not trust the leadership like I had in the past.

Even though Daddy and I were not on good terms, he did help me move. I was very hurt when he seemed to not care when he knew I did not have one piece of furniture to go into my apartment.

I did not have a bed or anything else. Because Daddy was angry with me concerning Miss Gloria, he just dropped me off at my new home. I slept on the floor for a few weeks. I was blessed to have $500. I asked Daddy to take me to the car auction. He had taken Cynthia, the girl he called his stepdaughter. Cynthia is Miss Ellen's youngest daughter.

Daddy took me to the auction to purchase a vehicle. Sadly, he did not fully check out the vehicle he chose for me. Without him checking to see if everything worked on the van, I went ahead and paid the first $500 for the vehicle. I had to submit the remaining $500 in two weeks. Daddy told me to go ahead and get the van and he would pay the other $500.

Two weeks came and went. When I called Daddy to remind him that Thursday would be the day to pay the remaining $500, Daddy told me he did not have $500 to give to me.

At that moment, I felt like: "I call you Daddy. You have done more for Cynthia than you have done for me in my lifetime." I felt in my heart: "All the cars you have brought for Cynthia at the auction were very dependable cars. You did not care about me. You picked a van for me that I would have to go through the passenger side to get in the van; part of the key was stuck in the ignition; the van had a bad oil leak."

Miss Gloria really helped me during this time. I was being drawn more and more to her. She took me to a furniture store and put a down payment on a living room set, a dining room set, and a bedroom set. Her daughter, Brook, brought all the things I needed like towels, pots and pans, silverware, etc. Miss Gloria paid $300 every month, plus I paid $200 towards my account.

Miss Gloria told me not to worry about when I got her money back to her. She was even going to purchase a nice vehicle for me. I was so embarrassed when I drove the van to her nice residence. It leaked oil every time. Every time I moved it, there was oil. I started parking the van on the side of her house.

While I worked at her school, Miss Gloria paid me in cash. I enjoyed working with the children. Miss Gloria could not go to the Jehovah's Witness Kingdom Hall because of some dispute she had with one of the leaders. They dismissed her from the Hall. The teacher came every Wednesday evening to do Bible Study with Gloria at her home.

I let Gloria convince me on some of her Wednesday night Bible Studies to sit and listen to the teacher so I could learn the truth. Many nights, I did not stay at my apartment; I spent the night with Miss Gloria.

Miss Gloria decided one evening to take me to an adult store and buy a vibrator for me. We also stopped to buy some wine while we were out. Miss Gloria was the first person to introduce me to vibrators for sexual pleasure. This was the first time I had seen a vibrator. She was shocked that this was my first time. Miss Gloria had promised that she was going to take me to a place and buy one for me. And she did.

This was my first time in the Adult Store. I knew in my spirit that this was wrong. My mouth was wide open as I saw the types of things people used for sexual pleasure. I felt so convicted, part of me wanted to go outside and sit in the car. She thought the way I was acting was extremely cute and funny. Miss Gloria took me to see the different sizes of the gadget she was going to purchase for me. I just wanted to get this over with and get out of that place.

Miss Gloria led me to the vibrators. I had never seen so many sizes and shapes of those plastic items. Miss Gloria picked out the same one for me that she had at home. I was so glad when she paid for the item and we left the store.

We made it back to her house. She poured some wine and asked if I wanted some. I told her no; she poured a glass for me anyway. We went into her room with our drinks. She opened the bag and began showing me how to use the vibrator. I decided to drink another glass of wine. Before long, I had consumed the whole bottle. I was a little on cloud nine. Remember that between the ages of 14 and 16, I drank vodka and Wild Turkey straight from the bottle, nothing added. I was an alcoholic at the age of 14.

Not only was I drinking with Miss Gloria, I had also started using profanity. I went to the room I normally slept in. I lay down for a while, still on cloud nine. I turned around, wobbling toward Miss Gloria. I asked if I could sleep with her that night.

She said, "Yes: as long as you behave."

I told her, "Oh, yes: I will behave." That night, we became more than friends.

James 1:14 – 15 AMPC [14] *But every person is tempted when he is drawn away, enticed and baited by his own evil desire (lust, passions).*

[15] *Then the evil desire, when it has conceived, gives birth to sin, and sin, when it is fully matured, brings forth death.*

The next day, I realized what I had done. I went into my room and cried, repenting, asking God to please forgive me.

I do not want to do this, but I cannot beat this thing.

Even though I did all that crying and repenting, I still did not separate myself from Miss Gloria.

Miss Gloria had a sister, Martha, who lived in a nursing home and was sick. Miss Gloria decided to bring her to live with her because she had cancer. I stopped going to work at the school and stayed at Miss Gloria's house to take care of her sister, day and night.

Miss Gloria took really good care of me. In turn, I took really good care of Martha. I would wake up in the middle of the night, clean Martha, and turn her on to her other side.

I did this for three months because I was in love with Miss Gloria. In the middle of one of the nights while I slept, Martha passed away.

I took it hard because I had become close to Martha while caring for her. Before she moved into Miss Gloria's house, I had visited her in the nursing home with Miss Gloria. During our visits, we would pick up Martha's clothes, wash them, and return them during our next visit.

After Martha's funeral service the next week, I returned to my house.

I began masturbating with the vibrator Miss Gloria purchased for me. I threw the toy in the trash out of frustration the next day. I don't know if it was God Who would not allow me to get any pleasure from that toy or not. I received no pleasure from its use.

Miss Gloria and her daughter Brook decided to take a trip to Texas. While she was gone, she gave me instructions to watch the school.

I had bad allergies. Those allergies required that I took a shot every morning. When she was around, Miss Gloria normally injected me. I tried to give myself the shot while she was gone, but could not get it right. I went to the school and asked the cleaning lady to help me. She told me she did not know how to give shots.

Miss Gloria and Brook returned from their trip. When they returned, I had many gifts for Miss Gloria. When she and Brook went to the school, the cleaning lady told Brook that I asked her to give me a shot in my breast as though I was making a pass at her.

Brook told her mother about the conversation, but she did not want her mother to tell me what had been insinuated. They were going to just watch me.

Out of jealousy, Miss Gloria called and told me what had been said. I told her that it was a lie; that I had only asked her to give me a shot in my arm.

I had forgotten that the cleaning lady was mad with me for telling Miss Gloria about how she was only halfway cleaning the school. I was so angry with her! I wanted to approach her about the lie.

I was in the classroom with three of my students when Brook came in to talk with me. She told me she had asked her Mama not to tell me about the conversation with the cleaning lady, but Miss Gloria told me anyway. I told Brook that, although I wanted to beat the mess out of the cleaning lady for lying on me, I would do nothing like that.

Brook shared with me that Miss Gloria had said I had been trying to hit on her. I was so hurt! I thought Miss Gloria cared for me. I discovered that day that all of it was a lie. Even though Brook said to just leave it alone, I wanted a meeting. Brook said OK and set up a meeting with Miss Gloria, Diana the cleaning lady, and me.

I could not believe what I was hearing during this meeting. It felt as though they had all come together against me!

Diana said, "You all said she likes women."

Brook said, "You did try to come on to Mama. So, this is all your own fault."

They wanted me to apologize to Diana and to Miss Gloria for bringing this mess into the school. So many thoughts rushed through my mind: how I had taken care of Martha; how I came for the summer and helped clean her school; how she had asked me to sign a check for her and assured me that if it was returned, she would have my back.

All I could think was, "This is how you treat me because of this cleaning lady?"

Tears rolled down my face. I walked out of that office never to return. The next morning, I needed gas. I wanted Miss Gloria to pay me for the days I had worked. She told me to come to the school and get the money. She thought it was all funny.

I trusted Miss Gloria. I did not realize that she was dirty inside and out. I had been blinded by sin. I could not see the real devil.

I am reminded of a man in the Bible: Samson. Samson allowed his flesh to control him. In the same way Samson's sin led him to spiritual blindness, my sin also led me to spiritual blindness. I continued to sin against God by trusting in my own strength.

Galatians 5:16 – 17 ESV *[16]But I say, walk by the Spirit, and you will not gratify the desires of the flesh. [17]For the desires of the flesh are against the Spirit, and the desires of the Spirit are against the flesh, for these are opposed to each other, to keep you from doing the things you want to do.*

Recurring sin is difficult to break. This is especially true when we continually submit to sin rather than to God: we give it power. God does not leave us in a permanent state of darkness, however. He has given us truth in His Word. We can use His Word and His power to combat these desires and share in His victory over sin and death.

I called Gloria to ask why she had told her daughter those things about me. She cussed at me and asked me why I had brought that mess to her job. I repeatedly told her that Diana had lied concerning what had really happened. I really didn't know what Diana had said I had done.

I told Gloria that I had trusted her, and she had betrayed me. I asked her how she could be so cold toward me after all the good I had done for her.

I asked, "Why didn't you tell the whole story?"

She hung up on me.

Every day, I called her. Every day, she cursed me out. Through all of this, I finally discovered that Miss Gloria was seeing a psychiatrist:

she had some mental problems.

I finally stopped calling her. She wanted me to apologize to Diana; that was not going to happen.

Brook came over to my place to do my hair. While she was there, we talked. She invited me to her house for a party.

I told her, "No, I cannot come."

I repented to Brook for living a double life with them. I asked her to forgive me. I hope she won't count it to God if she ever decides to ask Jesus into her heart. We hugged. I haven't seen Brook since that day.

Chapter 19

The Believer's Two Natures

Romans 7:15 – 25 ESV ¹⁵ *For I do not understand my own actions. For I do not do what I want, but I do the very thing I hate.*

¹⁶ Now if I do what I do not want, I agree with the law, that it is good.

¹⁷ So now it is no longer I who do it, but sin that dwells within me.

¹⁸ For I know that nothing good dwells in me, that is, in my flesh. For I have the desire to do what is right, but not the ability to carry it out.

¹⁹ For I do not do the good I want, but the evil I do not want is what I keep on doing.

²⁰ Now if I do what I do not want, it is no longer I who do it, but sin that dwells within me.

²¹ So I find it to be a law that when I want to do right, evil lies close at hand.

²² For I delight in the law of God, in my inner being,

²³ but I see in my members another law waging war against the law of my mind and making me captive to the law of sin that dwells in my members.

²⁴ Wretched man that I am! Who will deliver me from this body of death?

²⁵ Thanks be to God through Jesus Christ our Lord! So then, I myself serve the law of God with my mind, but with my flesh I serve the law of sin.

If I am saved, why do I still sin?

Why do I have such a problem with sin while I am here on Earth?

Why am I still troubled with impure thoughts?

Why do I sometimes do what I know is wrong?

Why do I sometimes fail to do what I know is right?

Why do I continue to battle with temptations?

Why do I sometimes live and act like an unsaved person even though it grieves and saddens me when I live this way?

1 Corinthians 3:3 ESV *for you are still of the flesh. For while there is jealousy and strife among you, are you not of the flesh and behaving only in a human way?*

Let's talk about the Old Nature. As believers who would be truly spiritual, we must recognize the fact that, within us, there are two natures:

- ➤ **The fallen nature of Adam...**
- ➤ **The perfect nature of Christ, begotten of God through the power of the Holy Spirit.**

No matter how we try to suppress these thoughts, these two natures are in every believer.

The Apostle Paul gives us his personal experience in **Romans 7**.

He tells us in **Romans 7:14, 25 ESV** that, on the one hand, *I am of the flesh, sold under sin.* On the other hand, though, *I myself serve the law of God with my mind, but with my flesh I serve the law of sin.*

Paul goes on to say in **Romans 7:18 ESV** *For I know that nothing good dwells in me,* and then tells readers in **Romans 7:22 ESV** *For I delight in the law of God, in my inner being.*

Paul is telling us here that the old nature and the new nature dwell within one person.

The "me" in verse 18 refers to the old nature; the "I" in verse 22 refers to the new man. We as believers must recognize the presence of the two natures within us.

The old man is called:

The flesh,

The old man,

The natural man,

The carnal mind.

In our flesh, we cannot please God because nothing good dwells in our flesh. (**See Romans 8:8**) Our flesh is totally depraved. God calls it sinful flesh. (**See Romans 8:3**) The sinful flesh always seeks to do wrong, and the works of the flesh are all bad (**See Galatians 5:13, 19 – 21**).

In respect to our flesh as believers, Apostle Paul declares that nothing good dwells in the flesh (**See Romans 7:18**) because it is "carnal, sold under sin" (**See Romans 7:14**). This is corrupt according to the deceitful lusts (**See Ephesians 4:22**) of our flesh. Our flesh is also *enmity against God and is not subject to the law of God; neither, indeed, can it be.* (**See Romans 8:7**)

Our flesh, as it remains in us as believers after salvation, is still the old, Adamic nature. It is sinful! Our flesh cannot improve or be changed. *That which is born (begotten) of the flesh is flesh*, our Lord said in **John 3:6**. No matter how hard a person tries, their flesh cannot be improved.

The flesh, or the old man, was dealt with over 2000 years ago on the Cross at Calvary. Scripture tells us to reckon him dead; therefore, put him off. Adam was created in the image and likeness of God. Unfortunately, he fell into sin and later produced after his own kind. **(See Genesis 5:3)**

Romans 8:3 – 4 KJV [3]*For what the law could not do, in that it was weak through the flesh, God sending his own Son in the likeness of sinful flesh, and for sin, condemned sin in the flesh:*[4] *that the righteousness of the law might be fulfilled in us, who walk not after the flesh, but after the Spirit.*

It is with respect 'to the flesh' in the believer, even in himself, that the Apostle declares that in it *dwelleth no good thing* **(See Romans 7:18);** that it is *carnal, sold under sin.* **(See Romans 7:14)** Paul declares that it is *corrupt according to the deceitful lusts* **(See Ephesians 4:22),** and that it is at *enmity with God* and *not subject to the law of God, neither indeed can be* **(See Romans 8:7).**

As we discovered with Adam, Fallen Adam could only generate and beget fallen, sinful offspring. These offspring could not even be changed by the law. But...

Romans 8:3 ESV *For what the law could not do, in that it was weak through the flesh, God sending his own Son in the likeness of sinful flesh, and for sin, condemned sin in the flesh...*

Chapter 20
Complete Deliverance

Miss Gloria stopped paying for my furniture. The company came and picked up all the furniture in my house. I only had one chair that my sister had given to me when I first moved into the apartment. Other than that chair, the apartment was empty. All I had was my kitchen utensils, bath towels, and clothes.

I was running out of the bare necessities. I used dishwashing liquid to take a bath. I did not have anyone to call for help.

God will not expose you until you refuse to turn from your sin. The devil is an Indian-Giver: he always comes back and takes his stuff!

I could not blame anyone for all the things happening to me. I knew it was the Hand of the Lord dealing with me. I was still angry with Gloria for betraying my trust and taking a stranger's word over mine. To be honest, it was not even her fault. I knew better; I knew what I was getting into and allowing into my life.

I realized that God allowed everything to happen in the way that it did. It did not matter how many times I cried over my sin; I kept on yielding to the sin.

Hebrews 12:6 AMPC *For the Lord corrects and disciplines everyone whom He loves, and He punishes, even scourges, every son whom He accepts and welcomes to His heart and cherishes.*

This passage also refers to **Proverbs 3:11 – 12 AMPC** *¹¹My son, do not despise or shrink from the chastening of the Lord* [His correction by punishment or by subjection to suffering or trial]; *neither be weary of or impatient about or loathe or abhor His reproof, ¹²for whom the Lord loves He corrects, even as a father corrects the son in whom he delights.*

Throughout the Bible, God shows Himself as a Father. Those who have received Jesus as Savior are His children. **(See John 1:12; Galatians 3:26)**

God uses the analogy of father/son because we understand that relationship. He compares Himself to a loving father who not only blesses but disciplines His beloved children for their own good. Hebrews 12 goes on to show that those who do not receive God's discipline are not legitimate children. **(See Hebrews 12:8)**

A loving father carefully watches his son. When that son disobeys God's Word and heads for danger, the father disciplines him to keep him safe. God does that with us.

When a born-again child of God heads for sin or refuses to resist temptation, our Heavenly Father brings chastening into his life to direct him back to holiness.

God's chastening can come in many ways: guilty feelings, unpleasant circumstances, loss of peace, relationship fractures, or any number of negative consequences for choosing sin.

There are many examples of chastening found throughout the Bible.

The Israelites continually disobeyed God's commands. **(See Numbers 14:21 – 23; Judges 2:1 – 2; 2 Kings 18:12)** He was patient with them. God sent prophets to plead with them; He warned them many times.

Unfortunately, the Children of Israel kept going after the idols and gods of the heathen. I did the same with my sinful lusts.

God chastened them through plagues or enemy attacks. **(See Jeremiah 40:3)** God still loved His children. In His love, though, He could not allow them to continue in the behavior that would destroy them.

In the same way, God could not allow me to continue in a lesbian lifestyle. God knew that if I did, in the end, it would send me to hell for eternity. God wanted me to turn from my wicked ways. Therefore, He allowed many things to occur in my life so I would be drawn to Him and turn from my sin.

Daddy had remarried by this time. One morning, his wife, Miss Princess, called me very early. She said she had not been able to sleep because of a disturbing dream about me. She told me she had shared the dream with Daddy and told him she was going to give me a call.

She asked me point blank, "Why are you sleeping on the floor?"

I told her, "I do not have a bed because I can't afford to keep paying the bill since I don't work for Miss Gloria anymore."

Miss Princess told me she was in the hospital. She wanted me to go to Jay's Resale Shop on Dell Hive Street. He sold mattresses, box springs, and bed rails.

"When you find a mattress, box spring, and rail, call me and let me know the price so your Daddy can have the money ready when you get here to the hospital," she told me.

I went to Jay's Resale Shop and found a bed, box spring, and bed rails. I called Miss Princess and told her the total of what I had chosen. The total was $150.

She told me she was in Room 225. "Your Daddy will give you the money when you come to the hospital."

When I got there, I knocked on the door. She told me to come in. Dad had left before I got there. I believe he was still angry with me about Miss Gloria.

I sat and talked with Miss Princess for about 30 minutes. I left and headed back to Jay's Resale Shop. Mr. Paul helped me put the bed and box spring on top of my van. He securely tied the rope across the top of the van and through the window.

The Resale Shop was not far from where I lived. I drove slowly so I could make it all the way to my apartment. I had no one to help me unload the bed and box spring from my van. I untied the rope. Taking my time, I slid the mattress off the top of the van; then, the box spring. I brought them both into the house.

I did not have a bed frame, but that was not important. All I knew was that I did not have to have my breasts burning anymore.

I put the rail together, added the box spring, and then the mattress. I cried tears of joy. Prior to this incident, I had never really known how much my God loved me. This was probably the first time in all my time of being saved that I had known His true love for me.

He took the time to tell Miss Princess, a woman I barely knew, to tell me to go and get a bed. All that time I had been without furniture, I never complained. I felt like I deserved everything that had happened to me. Thank God! He knew all of this would lead me back to the foot of the Cross. Not only that: the Father knew that total deliverance was coming into my life.

I began to fast, study the Word of God, and pray. Many nights, I had sat on the floor, my back against the wall, in prayer all night. When I could not stay awake, I tried to sleep on the floor. I could not get comfortable. Because of the size of my breasts, they would hang, causing me to get carpet burns.

On the last Sunday in November, I was so excited to go to church to tell my testimony of how much my Father loved me. I had to lead a song on that Sunday. The song I had to sing was perfect because it talked about God's love.

I began to tell them the reason I was sharing my testimony...

"I am not telling my testimony for anyone to feel sorry for me, but to rejoice with me because of what I have learned about God's love. For two weeks, I had nowhere to lay my head. I had been sitting up night and day, my back against the wall, because I did not have a bed to sleep on. I had told no one my situation.

"But God caused a woman I barely knew...my Daddy had just mamrried Miss Princess. Miss Princess told me that for two days, she had not been able to sleep because she had a disturbing dream that I was sleeping on the floor. While I was praying night and day with my back against the wall, God put me on Miss Princess' mind and told her to call me.

"Early Friday morning, Miss Princess called me and asked me, "Why are you sleeping on the floor?"

"I told her that I was not working with the school anymore and I could not afford to pay the bill for my furniture. She told me to go to Jay's Resale Shop. I'm sure some of you know about Jay's Resale Shop."

I continued with my testimony.

"When night came and when I got in that bed, I did not know that it had a dip in the middle. So, I had to sleep to the left or I would dip in the middle.

"I was so overjoyed! How much God loved me! I felt like I was sleeping on a Sealy Posturepedic Mattress."

Then I began to lead the song with the choir. Some in the congregation were crying; some were shouting. Most importantly, though, I gave God everything I had and praised Him like I had lost my mind. I was also excited that during the first week of December, I was getting on a bus to go back to Houston to be ordained.

After church, some of the Saints came up to me and put money in my hands. I went home and fell by the bed. I cried out to God. I prayed for total deliverance. I wanted the cycle to stop. I was tired of falling and getting back up saying, "I'm not going to engage in this activity again."

This was not my first visitation with God. A reverential fear came all over me when I heard His voice. I put my hand over my head to cover up because I knew I was in the presence of a Holy God. I did not move or say a word.

His voice was stern. He told me that I did not have to keep giving into this sin.

I said to Him, "I cannot beat this. It's stronger than me."

The Lord spoke the Word to me from **2 Peter 1:2 – 4 KJV** *²Grace and peace be multiplied unto you through the knowledge of God, and of Jesus our Lord, ³according as his divine power hath given us all things that pertain unto life and godliness, through the knowledge of him that hath called us to glory and virtue: ⁴whereby are given unto us exceeding great and precious promises: that by these ye might be partakers of the divine nature, having escaped the corruption that is in the world through lust.*

I never lifted my face from the floor as I heard Him sternly speak to me.

He said, "I have given you everything you need to walk in victory. *Now Choose You This Day. Who Will You Serve?*"

My head was still on the floor, tears rolling down my face. I could not stop trembling. I knew I was in the presence of my Lord and Savior, Jesus Christ. I felt unworthy to be in the presence of a Holy God.

With reverential fear in my voice, I said, "Jesus! Jesus, I choose You! I choose YOU!"

I knew then that every demon that had tormented my mind for all those years had to flee. I felt the weight lift off my shoulders. There was no doubt in my mind: Jesus had set me totally free!

Chapter 21

Healing the Real Man

(The Wounded Spirit)

Every relationship I had had with females was with women who were a few years older than I was. They were already established in life. Some had been married; some were still married with homes, jobs, etc. Satan knew that I longed for the love of a mother. In the female relationships I had, the need of a mother was met.

For example, you look at a beautiful lake. It doesn't appear to be deep. But once you decide to walk into the lake, you find out that it is not as shallow as you thought. Then you find yourself going under.

I was in a Wednesday Night Bible Service at Lily of the Valley Apostolic Church. Pastor Jones was ministering to different ones in the service. Pastor Jones looked at me.

She told me, "Sister Carla, you must forgive your parents."

In my mind, I said to myself, "She missed this one. She can't be talking to me. I have already forgiven my parents."

Pastor Jones said, "The devil did that to you. You must forgive."

My eyes became heavy with tears. I tried everything not to cry. I wondered to myself, *Why are you crying?*

I could feel the pain and hurt in my heart as she talked to me. I couldn't stop the tears as she continued ministering to me.

I said to myself, "I thought I forgave them."

That night, I realized I hadn't forgiven them. Pastor Jones continued ministering to me.

She said, "You can't go back looking for a mother. You missed that as a child. You must allow God to be your mother and your father. Scripture says, *My father and mother may abandon me, but the Lord will take care of me."* **(Psalm 27:10 GNT)**

Longing to be held by my mother and for her to tell me she loved me was my soul's desire in life.

Even though God had given me many fathers, mothers, sisters, and brothers in the Body of Christ, I always longed for my own family...despite the Body of Christ always making me feel like a part of their family.

I would hang around for a hot second with the Body. When someone asked, "Where is Carla?" They knew I had isolated myself in my room because that wasn't my real family.

I must be honest: God's not through with me yet. If the Body of Christ would be totally honest, we would see that we have a lot of wounded children trapped in adult bodies. It is important that we deal with childhood issues. If not, sooner or later, God is going to allow those childhood issues to surface. From the pulpit to the back door, we have a bunch of whining babies that have never dealt with their childhood issues!

Have you listened to the Body of Christ lately?

"She doesn't like me!"

"He didn't speak to me today."

"I can't get along with so-and-so. I don't need them! Who needs their friendship?"

"If it wasn't for my Mama or Daddy, I would not have made these bad choices in my life!"

It all boils down to childhood issues. It is important that leaders begin to learn and understand how to heal the total man: Spirit, Soul, and Body.

In their book, **Healing the Wounded Spirit,** John, and Paula Sandford state that, given that almost no one thinks in terms of daily feeding the personal spirit, the rule is that in those families where much prayer and tactile affection regularly occur, children are less starved or wounded. In those families where there is little of this, or none, children's spirits grieve and starve. Their inner spirit is angry and hurt, whether the mind and heart are aware of it or not.

When we discover that the adult to whom we are ministering was raised in such a home, we ask the Lord to find that starving inner child and take him into His own loving arms. We ask God to restore to him as many years as the canker worm has eaten and the locust destroyed. **(See Joel 2:25)**

This prayer has full scriptural warrant, for my father and my mother had forsaken me, but the Lord took me up. **(See Psalm 27:10)**

I was this child trapped in an adult body. I was still longing for a mother and father. Was I aware that my longing for love from my parents had caused me to make bad choices, decisions that were not healthy for my Spirit, Soul, and Body?

My longing had led me down paths that were physically and mentally abusive. The abuse brought upon other demonic spirits. Something I have learned in life is that you can't run from your past. Sooner or later, you will have to deal with the childhood issues that keep bringing you to those dark places.

Instead of me celebrating when I saw other parents giving their children love, the spirit of anger would rise in me.

When Pastor and Sister Boyd's children didn't clean their rooms like they were told or take out the trash before it overflowed, I had problems with that! And yet, I saw their parents express so much love toward them and toward me!

I could hear this loud voice inside of me saying, "Beat them! They don't deserve love; they deserve a beating!"

Why? Because that was what I was accustomed to. The way I dealt with children was the same way my parents had dealt with me. No one sat down and just talked to me like I had watched other parents do with their children.

In my time, you did what you were told to do without any questions. Expressing your feelings was not taken into consideration. If you didn't do exactly what you were told to do, you got a beat down with sting cords, fan belt, tree limbs; or steel-toed boots were thrown at you.

At one point, I was tied to the bed or to the willow tree outside and beaten by my Mama. All I could feel during those times was anger. I felt like I was treated like an animal. I was a teenager when those incidents happened to me.

Why didn't I feel close to Mama? Why don't I feel a Mama/Daughter bond?

When trouble and pain came my way, I reached out to the only people that showed me love, whether in the house of God, or in the world. I didn't set out to engage in this type of lifestyle; neither did I seek to find women to have relationships with. Only God knows the truth. I needed to be loved. Mostly, though, I desired to be loved by my Mama.

Even though I was a grown woman, many times, I just wanted Mama to grab me and tell me that she loved me. It was something I longed for on the inside: to hear from her.

Please allow me to identify it this way: the spirit of rejection is as cruel as the grave. There is a void and pain associated with the spirit of rejection. Not only do you feel the rejection of others, but a person will also oftentimes find they are rejecting themselves. I found myself rejecting me.

I often wondered why my life turned out the way it did. What did I do wrong to deserve the pain I felt inside? Why didn't my parents protect me from all the hurt, disappointments, pain, and mostly the lonely days and nights? Why didn't they love me in the way a child deserves to be loved?

Was it my fault? Was I the child that should not have been born? Was I the one that should have died before I was given a chance to live?

Being rejected as a child is a deep wound. Only the Father, in the name of Jesus, can heal and deliver you out of that world of constant letdowns.

I don't believe Mama set out to sow the spirit of rejection into my soul. Mama was young and had six (6) other children besides me. Because she was young with all those children, this may have been the cause of the treatment that came from her.

By all of them being so young, I am sure they demanded Mama's attention. I was not a baby that demanded much attention. When you cleaned me, fed me, and laid me back in the crib, I never said a word. Carl, on the other hand, demanded attention all the time. Mama had to mostly carry him all the time.

The devil sowed seeds of rejection into my soul as a baby. Mama would have Auntie Pamela and her sister Julie help by occasionally babysitting us. Mostly, though, the responsibility was on Mama.

Chapter 22

My Stages of Deliverance

Colossians 2: 15 – 17 AMPC [15]*[God] disarmed the principalities and powers that were ranged against us and made a bold display and public example of them, in triumphing over them in Him and in it [the cross].*

[16] *Therefore let no one sit in judgment on you in matters of FOOD AND DRINK, or with regard to a feast day or a New Moon or a Sabbath.*

[17] *Such [things] are only the shadow of things that are to come, and they have only a symbolic value. But the reality (the substance, the solid fact of what is foreshadowed, the body of it) belongs to Christ.*

Luke 11:21 – 22 ESV [21]*When a strong man, fully armed, guards his own palace, his goods are safe;* [22]*but when one stronger than he attacks him and overcomes him, he takes away his armor and divides his spoil.*

What does it mean to **bind** the strong man?

In Mark 3, Jesus was dealing with some Jewish scribes who were accusing Jesus of being possessed by Beelzebul. Their dispute was urged by the prince of demons he was casting out of them.

Mark 3:22 ESV *And the scribes who came down from Jerusalem were saying, "He is possessed by Beelzebul," and "by the prince of demons he casts out the demons."*

The scribes were saying that the reason the demons were coming out was because Jesus was in partnership with them as their leader. Jesus disagreed with their dispute with planned common sense.

Mark 3:23 ESV *"How can Satan cast out Satan?"*

He then told them a story. Jesus first spoke of the principle of a divided kingdom which will not stand in verses 24 – 26. He then told them that no one can enter a strong man's house without binding him.

Mark 3:27 ESV *But no one can enter a strong man's house and plunder his goods, unless he first binds the strong man. Then indeed he may plunder his house.*

Jesus explained that Satan is the *strong man,* and that he is the one who enters in and steals from the house. Before Satan can enter a person's house, he must be invited in. Jesus was not in partnership with Satan as the scribes stated. Jesus came to the earth, which is essentially Satan's house **(See 1 John 5:19),** to bind Satan and steal his goods, which are the souls of men. **(See John 17:15; Luke 4:18; Ephesians 4:8)**

Satan is strong. He holds possessions that he protects. But Jesus is the One Who was and is stronger than the strong man. Jesus is the only One Who can bind the strong man and rescue us from his clutches. **(See John 12:31)**

I can only share my experience of how I was totally freed from the spirit of rejection. I know that many thought I would have said free from the lesbian lifestyle. But it all stemmed from being rejected.

The spirit of lesbianism was not the **root** of my problem; it was an *extension* of my problem. Why? Although it is extremely important that we deal with the **root** of the problems, it is often much easier to deal with the *extension* of the problem.

In their book, ***Pigs in the Parlor,*** Frank, and Ida Mae Hammond quoted: "The door for the spirit of rejection to enter is most frequently opened during childhood, and even while a baby is still in the mother's womb. When a child is unwanted, the fetus is opened for the entrance of a demon of rejection."

Satan delights in finding an Achilles heel for a target; he chooses the weakest moments in life to attack. When is a person most defenseless? Before he is born and during infancy.

This baby, known as Carla Beaver, grew up to be a full-grown woman throughout life experiences. Other spirits attached themselves to the root of rejection that flourished within me. In essence, I was a grown woman. Inside that body, though, was a wounded spirit.

In their book, **Healing the Wounded Spirit,** John, and Paula Sandford said: "In child-raising, one thing is more important than all others. Parents can succeed in feeding their children's bodies nourishing food, their minds good schooling, and their soul's sound teaching in the Word, and yet still fail miserably. If they do not give copious amounts of simple affection, their children starve. Affection is the without-which-nothing in child-raising."

Every child needs to be held in loving arms many times daily. Because we are incarnate beings, spirit touches spirit in every hug. His Spirit touches each in the embrace.

Matthew 25:40 KJV *And the King shall answer and say unto them, Verily I say unto you, inasmuch as ye have done it unto one of the least of these my brethren, ye have done it unto me.*

Jesus was speaking of every person. He resides in every person. His influence is made weak in the lives of many by their neglect or denial. He expresses Himself in power in others. But He is there in all. His love is love. When we act in love, His life flowing in us nourishes us in every embrace.

Here is a simple maxim: when affection is given in normal healthy ways, people's spirits stay whole and seek normal healthy ways of expression. When affection is not given, drives and urges express themselves in wrong ways.

The spirit sickens, seeking out wrong answers for right needs. True affection does not lead to improper sexual touch and embrace, but away from it. It is the rare touches of inadequate affection which turn into lust.

In wholesomely affectionate homes, all the forms of child abuse almost never manifest themselves. We do not need to fear touch, only the absence of it. When children have not received enough affectionate touch, it is the task of counselors and the Body of Christ to heal.

Affection given to a 50-year-old can warm the heart of the 5-year-old within. When questions in counseling reveal starvation diets of affection, counselors need to pray with the person, enabling their inner child to forgive. Never mind that the person's mind may never have consciously identified resentment or anger.

Our personal spirit has a mind of its own. It has desires which, when they are thwarted, turn to anger.

It is to that inner spirit we minister when we ask the adult to say, "I forgive you, Dad and Mom, for not holding me enough."

When the counselee says the word – **forgiveness** – we should then pronounce that his inner child is forgiven, that sin of dishonoring his parents.

Never mind that in all his outward attitudes and sins of the heart, our Lord holds us accountable.

1 Samuel 16:7b ESV *"For the Lord sees not as man sees: man looks on the outward appearance, but the Lord looks on the heart."*

Matthew 15:19 ESV *For out of the heart come evil thoughts, murder, adultery, sexual immorality, theft, false witness, slander.*

Anger in the heart toward parents may be so well controlled, suppressed, forgotten, and overlaid with love and loyalty that they are thought not to be there. But that same anger may fuel perplexing explosions in other areas of our lives, towards mates, children, friends, employers, pastors, etc.

Chapter 23

God Remains Yet Faithful!

In this chapter, I want you to hear from my beloved, Brother Aaron Conley. God used him to play a huge role in me, turning my life around and finding love with him.

Aaron...

When I met Carla, I liked her more than I was willing to admit or accept. When I learned more of her story, I was shocked, of course, but I still desired to pursue her.

At the same time, though, I did not want to judge her. After all, we have all sinned and fallen short of the glory of God. No one is perfect. There were things in my life I had experienced that would show that I was not perfect in any way, shape, form, or fashion. But God...

I was very careful with how I responded to her concerning her past. I wanted to make sure I did not make any wrong responses because I did not want to offend her in any way. I didn't want to trigger anything inside of her that would cause her to have negative feelings about me, about us.

When we began seeing each other, we sought out the advice and counsel of our ministry leaders and those closest to us. No one really spoke against us coming into a relationship with each other. As a matter of fact, Sister Kathleen Boyd was very happy for us. She shared with us that she had felt that this was going to happen, that Carla and I would get together. Sister Boyd also indicated that God's will would be done through our connection. She told me that if her late husband, Apostle/Pastor Marvin T. Boyd was still alive, he would be so very happy for us. She even shared that he would give us his blessing to be married to each other.

As I see Carla growing into a beautiful, submitted wife, as I see the rough edges falling off her after being single for so long, I am Godly proud that God saw fit to bring us together and allow us to share our lives together. We both are willing to grow and make the best of our relationship with the help of the Holy Ghost.

Carla...

In 1999, the Spirit of the Lord spoke to me and told me that it was time to leave the church I had been serving in for over 20 years. My little sister was attending Faith Impact Full Gospel Church under the leadership of Pastors Marvin T. and Kathleen Boyd. One day, my sister invited me to attend the Faith Impact Ministry Sunday School.

The experience I had that Sunday morning was something that words could not explain. The place was packed from wall to wall. I never witnessed believers shouting for and dancing under the anointing of the Holy Ghost the way they did in that service.

The Sunday School teacher was on fire. She passionately taught in such a way that the people could not stay in their seats!

At that moment, I knew that this was the place for me. The Holy Spirit assured me that this was where I needed to be.

Brother Aaron Conley was already a member of Faith Impact when I joined. By the leading of the Holy Ghost, I joined the Faith Impact Family. Many came up to me and welcomed me to the family. Brother Aaron was one of those who shook my hand, welcoming me into the family.

I respected Brother Aaron in his calling as a minister and as a brother in the Lord. Over time, I realized that he was the type of man I desired God to bless me with. At the time, he was married. I saw so much of my Daddy in Brother Aaron. He was a hardworking man. A bonus, though, was that he loved God and the things of God.

At the same time, I realized that Brother Aaron was the type of man I wanted God to bless me with, it was also in my heart to run...for my life. I was scared because of all I had been through. And when you think about it, I had been single for a very long time.

During this time, there was one thing I would have done differently: I would not have allowed my guard to come down with Aaron: he was a married man. But I did.

All in all, Brother Aaron and I have a wonderful, Godly relationship. I acknowledge the fact and believe that we should have had more marriage counseling prior to getting married, though. Had we had more counseling, I, for one, would know how to better handle some of the things we are currently dealing with in our marriage. We both would be able to do a better job. But God...

While we were getting together and learning more about each other, some of the people in our lives had suggested that we needed more marriage counseling. They wondered why we were in such a rush to get married.

I must share with you the best advice I received from my ministry leader, the late Apostle Marvin T. Boyd. If he were alive today, he would tell me to submit myself to God so that it would be easier to submit to Aaron. His wife, Sister Boyd, shared with me to be kind, sweet, and always acknowledge God in everything we do. Another man of God I admire and respected told me that true love conquers anything. I have lived by these words and joyfully invited them into our marriage.

Please know this: I did not intentionally set out to hurt anyone in the past when I fell in love with Brother Aaron, but I did. I don't know why God honored the prayer concerning Brother Aaron I had prayed over 30 years prior to our coming together.

One day, I was praying. I knew it was wrong to covet someone else's husband, but I wanted to remind God of several things from His word. I brought to His attention that, even though David had slept with Bathsheba, she had gotten pregnant, David had her husband killed in battle, and there were consequences for David's sin, God still blessed David with Bathsheba and more.

I reminded God that He could do the same for me because I knew that He was not a respecter of persons.

My Pastors, Apostle Marvin T. and Sister Kathleen Boyd, came down to Texas from Colorado to do a revival. I allowed them to stay in my apartment while they were here. I stayed at my cousin's house. Apostle Boyd told me that he had begun to pray for me, but there was a war in the spirit for him to pray for me. He told me that several times as he began to pray for me, he sensed a spirit trying to hinder him from praying for me.

Pastor began to do warfare in the spirit until he broke through. The Spirit of the Lord began to speak to him concerning me. The Spirit of the Lord told him about my husband and how he was going to love me like I needed to be loved. He also told me that we were going to always dress alike and that this one thing was going to make my husband happy. All of this came to pass on July 13, 2022.

Author Bio

I am Carla Conley...

Carla Beaver was born on September 11, 1961, in New Orleans, Louisiana, during Hurricane Carla. As a result, she and her twin brother were named *Carl* and *Carla*.

Carla has a total of eight (8) siblings, of which six (6) remain: four sisters - April, Theresa, Almedia, and Tennile; and two brothers: Gilbert, and Christopher James. Carla's mother, Joyce Record, lives in Baytown, Texas. Her dad, James Williams, lives in Tulsa, Oklahoma.

Carla attended Drew Elementary and Drew Junior High School in Barrett Station, Texas. She graduated from Crosby High School in Crosby, Texas in 1979. Carla also attended online classes with Liberty University Christian College.

In May 1979, Carla received the baptism of the Holy Ghost with fire and the evidence of speaking in other tongues as the Spirit of God gave utterance. On October 23, 1979, Carla was serving under the leadership of Pastor G. and Sister O.B. Matthews at Shiloh Missionary Baptist Church in Barrett Station. Carla was dedicated and faithful to their ministry for over 20 years.

By the leading of the Holy Spirit, Carla was then led to join Faith Impact Ministry under the leadership of Apostle/Pastor Marvin T. and Sister Kathleen Boyd. She was appointed as their armor-bearer and served in their home and ministry for five years.

By her own admission, it took over 34 years before Carla was free and delivered from the spirit of *rejection*. Many would think Carla would have said the *lesbian* spirit. However, the lesbian spirit wasn't Carla's problem; it was an extension of her problem. Carla was active in the things of God but was defeated behind closed doors.

After many years of fasting, praying, and crying out to God for a companion, on July 13, 2023, God sent Carla a wonderful Man of God: Aaron E. Conley. They are still together in marriage and unity. They love each other totally and completely. With the help of the Lord, Aaron has helped Carla to see herself from a different perspective. He has helped her to see that God has her and is in control of all our lives.

Made in the USA
Columbia, SC
15 October 2024